teach yourself®

ballroom dancing
craig revel horwood
BBC's *Strictly Come Dancing* judge

foreword by len goodman

For over 60 years, more than
40 million people have learnt over
750 subjects the **teach yourself**
way, with impressive results.

be where you want to be
with **teach yourself**

Rehearsal facilities provided by the Jerwood Space.

 JERWOOD SPACE

The author and publisher take no responsibility for accident, injury or any other consequence of following the dances herein. Students practise at their own risk.

For UK order enquiries: please contact Bookpoint Ltd, 130 Milton Park, Abingdon, Oxon OX14 4SB. Telephone: +44 (0) 1235 827720.
Fax: +44 (0) 1235 400454. Lines are open 09.00–18.00, Monday to Saturday, with a 24-hour message answering service. Details about our titles and how to order are available at www.teachyourself.co.uk

For USA order enquiries: please contact McGraw-Hill Customer Services, PO Box 545, Blacklick, OH 43004-0545, USA. Telephone: 1-800-722-4726. Fax: 1-614-755-5645.

For Canada order enquiries: please contact McGraw-Hill Ryerson Ltd, 300 Water St, Whitby, Ontario L1N 9B6, Canada. Telephone: 905 430 5000. Fax: 905 430 5020.

Long renowned as the authoritative source for self-guided learning – with more than 40 million copies sold worldwide – the **teach yourself** series includes over 300 titles in the fields of languages, crafts, hobbies, business, computing and education.

British Library Cataloguing in Publication Data: a catalogue record for this title is available from the British Library.

Library of Congress Catalog Card Number: on file.

First published in UK 2005 by Hodder Education, 338 Euston Road, London, NW1 3BH.

First published in US 2005 by Contemporary Books, a Division of the McGraw-Hill Companies, 1 Prudential Plaza, 130 East Randolph Street, Chicago, IL 60601 USA.

This edition published 2005.

The **teach yourself** name is a registered trade mark of Hodder Headline.

Typeset by Pantek Arts Ltd, Maidstone, Kent.
Printed in Italy for Hodder Education, a division of Hodder Headline, 338 Euston Road, London NW1 3BH.

Impression number   10 9 8 7 6 5 4 3 2 1

Year   2010 2009 2008 2007 2006 2005

contents

foreword		**v**
acknowledgements		**vi**
CD track list		**vii**
introduction		**1**
commonly confused words		**2**
line of dance		**4**
abbreviations		**6**
what do I wear?		**7**
caution		**8**
warm-up		**9**
the holds explained		**12**
	ballroom holds	12
	latin holds	15
ballroom		**21**
01	**waltz**	**23**
	a little bit of wacky history	24
	what music do I dance to?	25
	floorcraft	25
	the basic waltz	26
	the steps	27
amalgamations		**38**
make up your own		**39**
02	**social foxtrot**	**41**
	a little bit of foxy history	42
	what music do I dance to?	42
	the steps	43
amalgamations		**53**
make up your own		**54**

03	**quickstep**	**57**
	a quick little bit of step history	58
	what music do I dance to?	59
	heel leads	59
	the steps	60
amalgamations		**74**
make up your own		**75**
04	**tango**	**77**
	a little bit of erotic history	78
	what music do I dance to?	79
	the steps	80
amalgamations		**91**
make up your own		**92**
latin american		**95**
05	**rumba**	**97**
	a little bit of raunchy history	98
	what music do I dance to?	98
	hot rumba action	98
	basic rumba	99
	the steps	100
amalgamations		**118**
make up your own		**119**
06	**samba**	**121**
	a little bit of sizzling history	122
	what music do I dance to?	122
	bounce!	124
	the steps	125
amalgamations		**146**
make up your own		**147**

07	**cha cha cha**	**149**
	a little bit of funky history	150
	what music do I dance to?	150
	the steps	151
amalgamations		**171**
make up your own		**172**
08	**jive**	**175**
	a little bit of jovial jive history	176
	what music do I dance to?	177
	how do I get the rhythm in my body and hands?	177
	the steps	179
amalgamations		**192**
make up your own		**193**
to wrap up		**194**
conclusion		**195**
taking it further		**196**
what dance when?		**198**
ballroom dance dictionary		**200**
bibliography		**205**
index		**206**

foreword

I first met Craig Revel Horwood when we were both judges on the BBC's *Strictly Come Dancing*. I had, of course, heard of him from his many West End shows that he has choreographed and directed.

When asked by Craig to read through his new book on Ballroom and Latin American dancing for beginners, I was filled with dread – not only for myself but for all those poor suckers trying to grasp the basic steps from all the technical jargon, intricate step patterns and complex timings. How wrong I was – this book is a joy. At last a chance to learn the basic moves in a clear, uncluttered way and not over technical but as Alex Moore (a famous dance teacher and inventor of the Whisk move in the Waltz) once said, 'The unambitious beginner need not be alarmed by the (to him) intricate details … they are as unnecessary to him as the intricacies of motor racing are to the ordinary car driver'.

Each dance has a potted history of its roots (making this book worth reading just for this!). The foot positions, alignments and amounts of turn are explained clearly – something that I have never seen in any book on dance technique before.

This is a most excellent book for the beginner, who is setting out on the road to ballroom and Latin American dancing success. It is an appetizer, giving the reader a taste of social dancing.

Good reading and happy dancing.

Len Goodman

acknowledgements

I really have to thank the incomparable Len Goodman – Head Judge, BBC's *Strictly Come Dancing* – for his incredible support and help putting this book together, and bringing a little more joy and many laughs along the way to the process. And equally his adorable and generous partner, Sue Barrett, for without her skill, patience and careful proof-reading and suggestions, none of this would make any sense and you'd all be doing 'flashdance' routines. Naturally, big hugs and kisses go to all the amazing dancers, the Latin couple Kerri Donaldson and Nuno Fernandes and the ballroom couple Lauren Addinall and Philip Hudson who all gave up their valuable time and bodies for the irreplaceable memories represented in the photos of these pages. Colin and Jackie Donaldson of Diamond Dancecentre for arranging the dancers for the shoot and for teaching their students so brilliantly. Lloyd Rooney for his love and total belief in me and support of every mad idea that crosses my mind, my family in Australia for putting up with the fact I'm always away and miss birthdays, The Imperial Society of Teachers of Dancing for keeping ballroom alive and regulated, Mr Rashmi Patel, Angela and all the staff at International Dance Shoes for the supply of shoes, our photographer, Niki Sianni and her assistant Dave Bentley, Jerwood Space for being the most friendly and glamorous studios in London to rehearse. Ross Mitchell of Dance and Listen Limited for all those cool tracks on the CD, Anthony Galatis at Uptown Studios for the recording, Catherine Coe and Lisa Collier at Hodder Education for telling me what's what! Joanne Osborn, the copy-editor who had a horrendous job but was as sharp as a tack and sorted it all out superbly, the design department for the fabulous footprints, the BBC for the *Strictly Come Dancing* TV series which undoubtedly created mass interest once again in ballroom dance and it's values. Last, but by no means least, the extremely brave celebrities that put themselves up for public humiliation and annihilation for one of the best causes in the world – dance education.

1	Copyright details	**14**	*Whatever Lola Wants*
2	My introduction	**15**	Rumba introduction – getting you started
3	Waltz introduction – getting you started	**16**	*Get Here*
4	*The Thorn Birds Theme*	**17**	*Goldfinger*
5	*Hushabye Mountain*	**18**	Samba introduction – getting you started
6	Social foxtrot introduction – getting you started	**19**	*Independent Women*
7	*Have You Met Miss Jones?*	**20**	*Axel F*
8	*Look What Happened to Mabel*	**21**	Cha cha cha introduction – getting you started
9	Quickstep introduction – getting you started	**22**	*Picture of You*
10	*Dancin' Fool*	**23**	*Hot Stuff*
11	*Don't Tell Mama*	**24**	Jive introduction – getting you started
12	Tango introduction – getting you started	**25**	*Soul Bossa Nova*
13	*Tres Hombres Paraglidos*	**26**	*Shake a Tail Feather*

'Yes, television will undoubtedly hasten the day in which the teaching of social dance takes its due place of honour and importance in the life of at least one entire nation'.

A. H. Franks, *The Ballroom Dancing Annual 1950*

I wanted to write this book in order to encourage people of all ages and abilities to get up and dance. The world seems to be full of couch potatoes! It's our job, now you have purchased this book, to make them stand up, learn to dance and get social. The rewards are enormous: you will burn major calories and have fun while you exercise.

What joy is there to be had from running nowhere on a running machine at the gym, when you could be spending time jiving instead of jogging, tangoing your tension away, waltzing your waist away, foxtrotting the fat off those hips and thighs, rejuvenating yourself with a raunchy rumba and quickstepping your way to meet new and interesting people? Social dancing is a great skill to have under your belt and it's not just an 'old person' thing – it's totally cool, funky and fantastically rewarding when you know how.

This book will help you to get a head start so that you don't feel embarrassed when you pluck up enough courage to go to your first dance class with real people. It is a great handbook to have to accompany your practical classes, and has invaluable style tips from the style guru expert, Len Goodman, to give you that professional look.

At the back of this book you'll find a CD on which I explain the rhythms and talk you through the basic moves of each dance. Each dance has two corresponding tracks for you to practise to so that you can get those moves up to speed.

As a director and choreographer, I have used all ballroom and Latin dances in this book as a base in many of my operas and West End London shows – *Spend, Spend, Spend, My One and Only, Copacabana, Guys and Dolls, Anything Goes, Calamity Jane, Beautiful and Damned, Pal Joey, La Traviata, Il Trovatore, Carmen*, just to name a few! These dances are not only used for the sheer beauty and entertainment value they provide, but also to signify a certain time, place and era, and to tell a story and help to move the plot along. Latin and ballroom have been used to great effect in many films and musicals. Think of *West Side Story*, cram packed full of mambo, cha cha cha, samba and jive or any of the Fred Astaire and Ginger Rogers movies which are all based on ballroom, waltz, quickstep, tango, foxtrot. Baz Lurhmann's movie, *Moulin Rouge*, has a wicked tango to the tune 'Roxanne', where Caroline O'Conner dances up a storm with a load of guys! Dance is a particularly powerful tool in which to convey emotion and, as more and more movie musicals are hitting our screens making dance more and more popular, it is our responsibility to know at least the basics. No one really wants to sit alone in a corner like a wallflower at a social event, too scared to dance. So come on, be brave and daredevilish – liberate yourself and take your first step into the decathlon of dance.

commonly confused words

There are a few commonly confused words in dance, and below we have explained these so that you can be confident that you will sound as if you know what you are doing when you start out.

alignment The direction that your body and feet are facing in relation to the room and to the all-important LOD (line of dance). It can also mean the direction of the movement. It's such a versatile word, as your body should have 'proper alignment', basically lining up all your different body parts so they can move harmoniously together and make you look fabulous!

ball Not a round object used in games or a formal social function, but a dance term used to describe the landing of body weight onto the ball of the foot – the padded area between the arch of the foot and the toes.

body weight Not the percentage of fat you have compared to lean muscle tissue, but a term we use to suggest that your weight can travel from one leg to the other by shifting your body weight through your centre.

brush The action of closing the moving foot to the standing foot without changing weight between steps, and certainly not the one you use for grooming your hair.

carriage Your carriage does await but won't turn into a pumpkin at midnight thankfully as this term relates to the position of the upper body whilst in dance position.

centre The invisible line that runs through the body which gives you your centre of balance; also refers to the centre of the room or dance floor.

control Without balance and stability throughout the body while you are dancing, your life in dance would be limited. You need great control over your body when you dance.

cucaracha A basic international figure consisting of side steps to the left and right. The move is named after one of my most favourite filthy, dirty insects, the cockroach! It's a useful 'holding pattern' dance until you decide what step may follow. It gets its name from the Spanish word, 'cucaracha' which means cockroach.

downbeat This isn't a mood swing, but simply refers to the very beginning of each beat. If a measure is counted 1 and 2 and 3 and 4 then the numbers 1, 2, 3 and 4 are considered to be the downbeats, while the 'ands' are the upbeats. It also refers to the strongest beats in each measure. In 4/4 music, the downbeats are the 1 and the 3; the upbeats are 2 and 4.

fan An enthusiastic admirer of a celebrity or public performer – also a basic figure used in the international style rumba and cha cha cha.

figure This is the name given to a standardized step pattern which, together with other patterns, constitutes the basis of a dance, and so it is nothing to do with how slim you are.

flat Not an apartment, but when the foot is flat to the floor.

footwork This means the part or parts of the foot used during a step.

frame The position of the arms and body in dance position. For example, in normal hold, the boy creates a frame that the girl moves into.

heel The part of the foot directly below the ankle and behind the arch.

hip action A good hip action is the result of good foot, ankle, knee and leg action – not the actual shaking or wiggling of the hips. The hip movement should occur naturally because of how your legs are moving.

instep This isn't an 'in' or 'fashionable' step, but is the part of the foot on the inside edge, between the ball and the heel.

leading and following The boy is responsible for leading from one figure to the next and it's the girl's job to follow.

measure As opposed to units of alcohol, this measure is a unit of music representing a group of consecutive beats. The number of beats in a measure is calculated by the time signature and determined by the ratio and relative strength of the naturally strong and weak beats occurring in the music.

poise The position of the body in relation to the feet.

posture The way in which you hold your body and carry yourself. Good posture is achieved by vertically aligning the head, shoulders, abdomen and hips.

quick A count which is equal to one beat of music, exactly half the time of a 'slow'.

rhythm This is the regular pattern of beats and emphasis in a piece of music – the pulse or beat created by the various musical and percussive instruments playing a piece of music. If you ain't got it, get it quick!

slow A count equal to two beats of music – exactly twice the time of a 'quick'.

swivel A turn on the ball of one foot.

toe One of the five wiggly things that hang off the end of your foot, the term is used to express what part of the foot is used at any one particular time, like 'lead with the heel, not with the toe'!

whip In dance terms this is a swing pattern that whips the girl from one side of the boy to the other and back again.

Note: There is a full ballroom dance dictionary at the back of the book (see page 200). A whole new language for you to discover – enjoy!

line of dance

You need to understand the Line of Dance (LOD) if you are not going to crash and burn, or travel up a one-way street and take out a few couples in the process. I know, it all sounds like great fun, but you and your partner will be thrown off the dance floor never to return if you don't follow this simple rule.

The LOD refers to an imaginary line that is drawn anticlockwise around the dance floor or room in which you are intending to dance. It's the motorway you'll be dancing down with lots of imaginary roads running off it. On your left is the 'centre' of the room, normally where the chandelier is hanging or fluorescent light fitting is fixed. When you have discovered the centre of the room, look to your right and you should see a wall of some description. That is called the 'wall'. Your motorway is the area between the centre and the wall. It is within this area that you will dance in an anticlockwise direction around the dance floor.

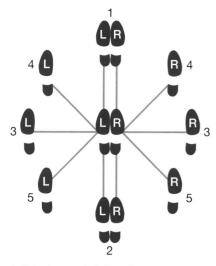

1 right foot or left foot forward
2 right foot or left foot back
3 right foot or left foot to the side
4 right foot or left foot diagonally forward
5 right foot or left foot diagonally back

figure 1 foot positions

There's plenty that you can do with the LOD, for instance you will find yourself facing the wall square on and this is called 'Facing Wall' (FW), or you might find yourself on a diagonal facing the wall – Diagonally to the Wall (DW). You can also face on a diagonal to centre – Diagonally Centre (DC). As you can see, all the directions that your body face come from this one rule – when facing the LOD, body angles are relative to the centre and the wall. The LOD, therefore, will be individual to each couple.

Once you understand the concept, the LOD and alignments will seem perfectly natural to you, particularly when you are physically in the space.

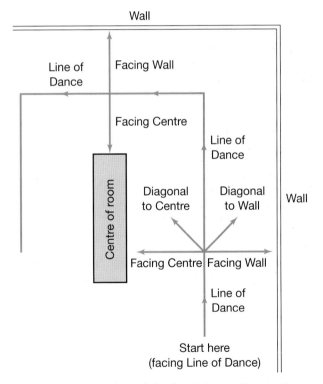

figure 2 the direction of the body in relation to the room and the Line of Dance

abbreviations

ABB	Alternative Basic Bounce
BB	Basic Bounce
BC	Backing Centre
BW	Backing Wall
C	Centre
CPP	Counter Promenade Position
DC	Diagonally Centre
DW	Diagonally to the Wall
FC	Facing Centre
FW	Facing Wall
L	Left
LA	Left Arm
LF	Left Foot
LH	Left Hand
LOD	Line of Dance
LRL	Left Foot Chassé (Left Foot, Right Foot, Left Foot)
OP	Outside Partner
PP	Promenade Position
R	Right
RA	Right Arm
RF	Right Foot
RH	Right Hand
RLR	Right Foot Chassé (Right Foot, Left Foot, Right Foot)
SxS	Side-by-Side position

Important!

I can't stress enough how important it is to get really familiar with your alignments – the north, south, east and west of ballroom dancing. You need to know the abbreviations almost backwards. Please study them in great detail until you are sick to death of them. I promise it will only make your study of dance more enjoyable and get you onto the dance floor quicker.

Throughout this book the following key is used in all figures. So girls, remember to follow the red footprints and boys, follow the blue!

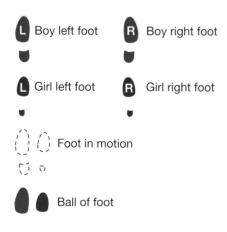

L Boy left foot   R Boy right foot

L Girl left foot   R Girl right foot

Foot in motion

Ball of foot

what do I wear?

Don't panic! You won't have to slip into a pair of tights and leg warmers but you will have to wear something that's suitable for dancing practice. It used to be (and in some schools still is) that the boy would have to wear a tie but I believe that is horribly old-fashioned and, when you're learning to dance, not the most comfortable accessory. The most important thing is to wear something that is comfortable and non-restrictive because your body needs to be able to move fluidly and without the constraints of ill-fitting jackets or tight clothing that limit your body movement. Jeans or any denim would not be appropriate as the material doesn't breathe or give in any way. As you are going to perspire, be practical and wear something sensible like loose-fitting light weight cotton trousers and shirt for the boys or a practice skirt and top for the girls that enable you to move easily. For the boys, it also helps to wear a T-shirt under your light weight shirt just to protect yourself from perspiration. And take a hanky for mopping your brow if you tend to heat up quickly.

Shoes are very important and there is a vast range of specialized dance shoes that offer support and comfort; you don't want blisters or worse to stop you from enjoying the whole experience. The shoes are not that expensive and, considering the many hours you will spend in them, are a wise investment. For the ballroom, the heel for the girl is smaller or lower than in the Latin dances, where the girls wear up to $3^{1}/_{2}$ inch heels. The boy also has a heel range of about 2 inches for Latin and tango. The shoes also come in a range of heights below that, but my advice would be to start with the lower heel until you become more familiar with the dances and have a pair of flat, comfortable shoes on standby in case the balls of your feet become tender. Comfort first, please! You will find the contact details for International Dance Shoes on page 197, offering a range of amazing shoes and fashionable clothes, specifically designed for dancing.

caution

A little word of caution before you get carried away! Before you attempt any of the dances in this book, consider your physical condition. If you have any physical pain prior to dancing or exercising for dance, please consult your physician before beginning. It is also very important to warm up the muscles before using them, and on pages 9–10 there are some basic warm-up techniques to prepare you for any of the ballroom or Latin dances.

warm-up

To begin

Stand up straight, pull your stomach in and squeeze your buttock muscles. Make sure your feet are apart at a distance just beyond the hips, and your knees are in line with your toes and slightly bent. Your shoulders should be relaxed but pressed down, and your arms should be by your sides and relaxed.

> **Note:** Don't forget to breathe deeply as you do these exercises.

Neck stretches

Tilt your head gently to one side, feeling the stretch down the side of the neck. Hold for a few seconds then recover. Then repeat on the other side and recover. Do this four times on each side. Then gently lower your head to your chest stretching the back of the neck (don't go too far, only go to where is comfortable). Hold for a few seconds and recover. Looking towards the ceiling, take your head up and hold for a few seconds and recover. Repeat four times. Look to the side and hold, then look to the other side and hold. Repeat four times.

Shoulder rolls

Lift your shoulders up slowly and hold. Then release down slowly and hold. Repeat eight times. Then roll your shoulders up and around to the back four times, then roll them forwards four times.

Elbow circles

Place your hands on your shoulders and circle your elbows backwards eight times, then forwards eight times. Release your arms slowly back by your sides and check your posture is still in the position in which you began.

Reaches

Slowly lift both arms up to the ceiling with your palms facing the front. Stretch up for a moment, then release slightly without bringing your arms down, and again up for a moment, and release. Do this four times. Then alternate right hand up then left hand up, feeling the stretch in your sides. Repeat this four times each side. Recover by bringing your arms down slowly and shaking your body out a little.

Hips

Stand with your feet apart, but not too far, equal with your hips. Your toes should be pointing straight ahead, and knees facing over toes. Place your hands on your hips and move your hips to the side then centre, then other side then centre. Do this eight times to each side.

Knee bends

Place your feet together in parallel with your toes pointing straight ahead. Your hands should still be on your hips and your knees should be over your toes, then slowly bend your knees a little, keeping a nice straight back, then recover slowly as you straighten them. Repeat eight times. It is important not to go too far down in this exercise. If you have trouble with your balance, you can hold on to the back of a stable chair or place your hands on a wall.

Ankle rolls

You may need to hold on to the wall or the back of a chair for this exercise as it requires that you stand on one foot. If you have problems with that, it can also be done seated.

Roll your ankle in an outward and around motion eight times, then reverse the motion inwards eight times. Repeat with the other ankle.

Toe raises

Stand facing a wall and put both hands on the wall to help support and control your balance. Your feet should be just a little apart and parallel, with your toes pointing towards the wall and your heels on the floor. Slowly rise up on your toes, then release down slowly through the foot, back to your heels. Repeat this eight times.

Hamstring stretch

Only do this move if you have no back injuries, lower back pain, and calf or hamstrings injuries.

Stand with your feet apart and in parallel with toes pointing straight ahead, as in the beginning position. Then slowly lower your head and very gently roll down through the spine as your arms lead to reach for the floor. Don't go too far, only to where is comfortable. If you feel any pain, stop. You should feel a gentle stretch of your hamstrings – the muscles at the back of your legs. Hold for a moment, then recover, rolling up through the spine back to your starting position. Repeat this four times, and don't forget to breathe deeply.

Tendon stretch

Let's go back to the wall as before and stretch out our Achilles tendons. Lean at a 45° angle against the wall, supporting your weight with your hands. Then place one foot flat to the floor in front of you, your knee should be bent and over the toe in front of you. Place the other foot behind you on to the ball of the foot, gently straightening the leg. Slowly lower the heel of the foot behind keeping the leg straight, feeling the stretch in the tendon. Hold for a moment then repeat on the other side. Do this four times.

Shake out

Shake out the body. Then, just to get the blood pumping around the body a little, try some small jogs on the spot to finish.

This is a very basic warm-up, and if you feel the urge to do an aerobic workout that you're used to or your favourite football-training programme, that is fine. The important thing is to warm-up in some way because most injuries are due to people's muscles being cold and not ready for action.

the holds explained

Ballroom holds

Normal hold front view of the boy

The boy's right arm is placed around the girl with his right hand above her waist and just below her left shoulder blade. The boy's left arm is in a raised position, bent at the elbow, and both elbows should be on a line just above the line of the waist.

Len's top tip

For the right-hand position feel for her bra strap!

Normal hold front view of the girl

The girl's left arm should be resting lightly on the boy's right arm near his shoulder, and her hands not clasping or clawing, but fingers together and relaxed. The girl places her right hand in the boy's left hand, between his thumb and index finger, and then positions her head looking over his right shoulder. The girl should be standing slightly on the boy's right side.

Side view beginner's hold optional

Here Sue and I demonstrate a great hold for practising new material. It is a wider hold, so when you're learning the steps you'll have less chance of stepping on each other's toes. It's also easier for your balance and control. The girl's arms are just resting on top of the boy's arms, creating lots more space between you.

Tango front view

Up close and very personal! As you can see, the boy's right arm is further around the girl, which in turn makes her stand a little more to his right side. The boy also needs to bring his left hand in towards himself, creating a more compact position. The knees are bent or 'flexed' and, to stop you banging your knees together, the right toe should be level with the instep of the left foot – see how Sue has her feet positioned, the boy's position should be the same. The girl needs to place her left hand on the boy's back below his shoulder, under the armpit with the palm facing the floor.

Promenade position (PP)

You both have to create a V-shape with your torsos. The boy is facing the front and the girl turns her body to the right slightly. Don't exaggerate this position, and make sure your bodies remain in contact with each other on the boy's right side and the girl's left side.

Outside your partner position (OP)

This is the position you should be in when the term is used 'to dance outside your partner' – one of Len's favourite positions. The boy takes his forward step on the right foot, outside the girl's right side (OP). His right foot should be placed directly in front of his left foot maintaining hold with the girl. So don't let go of her, boys!

Latin holds

Normal hold

You will be pleased to know that the Latin normal hold is just a looser version of the normal ballroom hold where your bodies are just a little more apart!

Open facing position

Left hand to right hand hold

In this hold you will be in an open position, a little apart from your partner. The boy takes the girl's right hand in his left hand, between his thumb and index finger, and the free arm is normally extended to the side at waist height.

Right hand to left hand hold

This is the same as the hold above, but the girl's left hand is held in the boy's right hand.

Double hand hold

In this hold the boy and girl are apart. The boy offers the palms of his hands to the girl and she places her left hand in his right hand and her right hand in his left hand.

Promenade position (PP)

In the Latin dances, the PP is slightly different to the ballroom PP because your bodies are just a little further apart and, when the term 'counter promenade' is suggested, the girl stands on the other side of the boy, on his left side.

Fallaway position

This is a cool position and it's used in the jive. It's a V-shaped position just like the PP, except you are both moving backwards. Len and Sue are pictured here in the fallaway position – having a whale of a time!

Change of hands behind back

This is used in the jive. It's where the boy's hands need to change behind his back. You can see here how this is achieved, and there is a full description of how to do it on page 188.

Left side-by-side

You will use this many times in the rumba and cha cha cha. It is also used in the jive! It's where the girl is on the boy's left side, with you both facing the same way.

Right side-by-side

This is the same as on the previous page but reversed, where the girl is on the boy's right side facing the same way!

Note: An optional hold for the rumba is the close contact hold or breath-mint position (see page 99 – only to be used if you feel very comfortable with your partner and you've just brushed your teeth!). It is safer to learn most of the moves in a wider position at first, just to give your toes a chance.

ballroom

waltz
social foxtrot
quickstep
tango

waltz

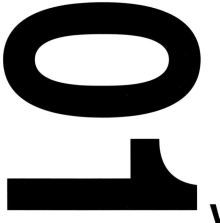

waltz

A little bit of wacky history

The waltz caused a riot back in the very early nineteenth century when man first, no, not walked on the moon, but placed his hand on the lady's back and danced in such close proximity that people thought it disgusting, disgraceful and downright degrading! Society would never be the same – how would it ever recover from this filth? Check out what *The Times* had to say.

We remarked with pain that the indecent foreign dance called the 'waltz' was introduced (we believe for the first time) at the English Court on Friday last. This is a circumstance, which ought not to be passed over in silence. National morals depend on national habits: and it is quite sufficient to cast one's eyes on the voluptuous intertwining of the limbs, and close compressure of the bodies, in their dance, to see that it is indeed far removed from the modest reserve which has hitherto been considered distinctive of English females. So long as this obscene display was confined to prostitutes and adulteresses we did not think it deserving of a notice; but now that it is attempted to be forced upon the respectable classes of society by the evil example of their superiors, we feel it a duty to warn every parent against exposing his daughter to so fatal a contagion … We owe a due reference to superiors in rank, but we owe a higher duty to morality. We know not how it has happened (probably by the recommendation of some worthless and ignorant French dancing master) that so indecent a dance has now for the first time been exhibited at the English Court; but the novelty is one deserving of severe reprobation, and we trust it will never again be tolerated in any moral English society.

The Times, Summer, 1816

Imagine what they would have said about Patrick Swayzee in *Dirty Dancing* or John Travolta in *Saturday Night Fever*. Lock up your daughters! Society soon got over it. The waltz became so popular because it was so much fun to dance to its 3/4 rhythm and fabulous first downbeat. People became intoxicated by it, and it was spreading like wildfire throughout the world. It originally started in Germany as a wooing dance, featuring a close embrace and lots of giddy turns. It also had a swing to it, which was new at the time, so you needed great balance otherwise you'd 'crash and burn', and that isn't a good look on the dance floor.

The French danced it on tip-toes, and the Viennese went mad with it. They danced it with a massive amount of speed and, because of their passion for speed, danced it on more of a flat foot, gliding and turning around the room while throwing their heads and bodies from one side to the other. Today, the waltz comes in two forms:

1 The modern (or diagonal/slow) waltz.

2 The Viennese (or quick) waltz.

It wasn't until the early 1920s that there was an agreement to find a uniform and basic step. In 1927, the Imperial Society's Ballroom Committee standardized ballroom dancing and adopted the diagonal waltz. This style became the basis of the dance, and is the one you will learn here.

What music do I dance to?

The time signature for the waltz is 3/4, which simply means it has three beats to every bar of music. That means you only count up to three, instead of four as in all the other dances. The downbeat or first beat of the bar is pronounced **1** 2 3, **1** 2 3, etc. The recommended tempo for the waltz is a comfortable 32 bars per minute.

Track list

3 My introduction – getting you started.

4 *The Thorn Birds Theme*

5 *Hushabye Mountain*

Why don't you listen to track **3** of the CD to see if you can hear that all-important first beat of the bar?

Floorcraft

You must have your wits about you if there are more people on the dance floor than you and your partner. Even if you're the only couple dancing, it can be dangerous because there are walls, tables, chairs and all sorts of other unexpected obstacles you both may crash into or slip on. This is why you need good floorcraft in order to dodge other couples or surprise obstacles while remaining in control and looking graceful. You also need to be able to anticipate in which direction other couples may go, and have a 'sixth sense' about which route they may take. Basically you must follow certain rules and go with the traffic flow:

- Don't dance on the wrong side of the centre line. You'll create chaos and havoc and will be the most unpopular couple at the ball.

- Give way to beginners – they are dangerous!

- Take action to avoid catastrophe. If you see a pile-up ahead, don't kamikaze and waltz into danger!

What's flow?

Go with the flow, not against it. The dance moves in an anticlockwise direction around the room. When I talk about the flow of traffic, I'm talking about the dancers' movement around the dance floor.

Take the corner

The thing about cornering is not to panic! It's actually very easy. When you arrive at the point of no return – the corner – all you do is look at the new wall ahead of you and change your orientation to that wall, working parallel with it. You will have also noticed that your centre line (the LOD) has changed to run parallel to your new wall, and that can continue for as long as there are walls, and as long as you have the energy to dance – days, even weeks!

The basic waltz

Elegant, elegant, elegant! That is what we need to remember. The waltz is a dance of elegant turns and gliding movements, moving effortlessly around the dance floor, not a big old drunken hoedown. It should be full of rise and fall.

Rise and fall?

Yes, rise and fall! As the term suggests, it's the up and down feeling of the movement as you move through the steps, and this is described as the natural swing of the waltz. This really is the most difficult thing to perfect as it requires lots of great balance and control, but with practice, you'll be the proud owner of a good swing action!

How do I rise and fall?

Rise and fall is like life, it's full of ups and downs but, unlike life, you can control when you are up and when you are down – that is the beautiful thing! In the waltz, you step forwards on the heel, then rise to the toe; start to rise up at the end of step 1, then continue to rise on steps 2 and 3, then at the end of step 3 you simply lower or fall back onto your heel again.

Sway

Do you want to look tense, stiff and wooden on the dance floor? I think not. So, you will need a little sway. Sway is really important because it gives the waltz its easy and relaxed style. Sway is simply the tilting of the body. What you do is sway away from the extending foot and sway towards the closing foot. It should feel quite natural and, if it doesn't, you must be doing the opposite of what I have just said.

The hold

Boys only! Girls, sneak a peek

The boy creates a 'frame' for the girl to step into, and it's this frame that will lead the girl around the dance floor. Good luck, boys!

It's easier, boys, if you practise the hold without your partner, just to get a feel for the basic frame. You need to look at what your feet are up to and start thinking about what's happening down below. Make sure your feet are together, and that your toes are facing straight ahead and not out to the sides like a duck. Hold your body straight up, not slumped. If you have a beer belly, pull it in; I call this pulling up! Now to test your balance, have a go at doing a few calf-raises by rocking and lifting up on your toes and down again onto your heels. Try that a couple of times, then deal with the arm positions.

Raise both arms to stop the traffic, then lower the right arm to just above the level of your waist as that's the one that's going to go around your partner and be placed under her right shoulder blade. Make sure the level of your left arm is correct. Your left hand should be approximately level with your eyes. This, however, is subject to your height; if your partner is extremely tall or short, you will have to adjust the levels to suit both of you. Now please look at 'The holds explained' on pages 12–13 so that you can copy them. Boys look at 'Front view of the boy', and girls look at 'Front view of the girl'.

Following the boy's lead

Now comes the worst bit for the girls. Whatever mess your partner makes of the dance, it's your responsibility to follow him, right or wrong! It shouldn't end in tears if you're both aware of one another and take equal responsibility for your weight and balance.

The girl should be equally aware that she must carry herself and her weight in such a way that doesn't make her partner feel like he is dragging her around the floor, with a 2-tonne weight strapped to her back.

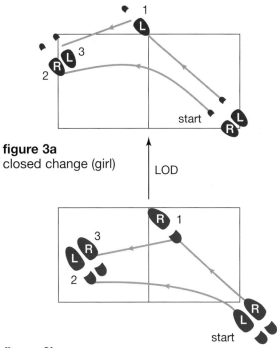

Len's top tip

In the waltz you need rise and fall

Step 1 on the heel, then the ball

You should learn to sway

To improve your display

For the right turn, commence diagonal wall

The steps

You will notice that I am including abbreviations, shorthand memory points, for example, Boy RF forward (right foot forward) and Girl RF back (right foot back) to make it easier to remember a sequence of steps. You can write these down on small cards to jog your memory; they are also internationally recognized abbreviations that you will need to learn as you progress in the sport (see page 5). It won't take you long to get used to the abbreviations, just be patient and don't try to rush. In a matter of minutes, you'll be rattling them off like a pro!

Points to remember

Natural turns always turn to the right, that's clockwise. Boys always start on the right foot and girls on the left.

Reverse turns always turn to the left, that's anticlockwise. Boys always start on the left foot and girls on the right foot.

Right foot closed change

These next three moves (the closed change step) are the fundamental basics you'll need to learn as a beginner. You can dance the right foot closed change and the left foot closed change steps one after the other. To practise them, dance them in a straight line down the room first, then try them with the alignments. The rhythm goes like this: 1, 2, 3.

Listen to track **3** on the CD where I will talk you through the right and left foot closed change.

Move 1 *count 1*

■ *Boy RF forward*

Start by facing DC with your weight on the left foot, and then walk forwards on the right foot.

figure 3a
closed change (girl)

LOD

figure 3b
closed change (boy)

■ *Girl LF back*

Start by backing DC with your weight on the right foot, and then walk back with the left foot.

Move 2 *count 2*

■ *Boy LF side*

Step sideways with the left foot.

■ *Girl RF side*

Step sideways with the right foot.

Move 3 *count 3*

■ *Boy RF closes to LF*

Close the right foot to the left foot.

■ *Girl LF closes to RF*

Close the left foot to the right foot.

Now follow directly with this next sequence of steps.

Left foot closed change

Just like the right foot closed change, this move has three steps and the rhythm goes like this: 1, 2, 3.

Move 1 *count 1*

■ *Boy LF forward*

Start by facing DW with your weight on your right foot, and then walk forwards with the left foot.

■ *Girl RF back*

Start by backing DW with your weight on your left foot, then walk backwards with the right foot.

Move 2 *count 2*

■ *Boy RF side*

Step sideways with the right foot.

■ *Girl LF side*

Step sideways with the left foot.

Move 3 *count 3*

■ *Boy LF closes to RF*

Close the left foot to the right foot.

■ *Girl RF closes to LF*

Close the right foot to the left foot.

Well done! You've been brave and just taken your first steps to waltzing wilfully. To practise this around the room, waltz together along the LOD and adjust the direction around the corners so you don't crash into the walls or furniture. You will learn how to take the corners properly with the next figure, the natural turn, but, for now, just concentrate on making it as smooth as you can. When you feel ready and you've stopped treading on one another's toes, go on to learn the natural turn. Don't rush learning any of the basics, it will be your downfall, and practise, practise, practise!

Natural turn

This figure is really useful to get you around a corner. You can dance your closed changes in a straight line down the side of the room then use a natural turn to take the corner.

Point to remember!

Natural turns always turn to the right, that's clockwise. Boys always start on the right foot, girls on the left.

This figure has a total of six steps and the rhythm goes like this: 1, 2, 3, 1, 2, 3.

Let me now introduce you to Philip and Lauren who will demonstrate and physically guide you through the natural turn.

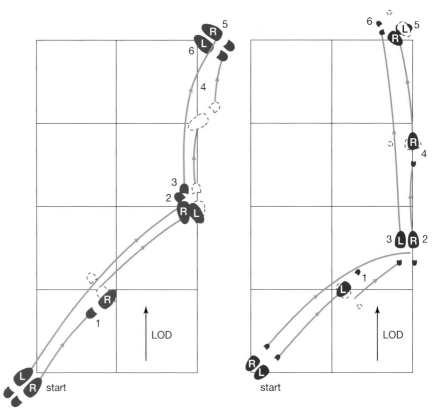

figure 4a natural turn (boy)   **figure 4b** natural turn (girl)

Move 1 *count 1*

■ *Boy RF forward*
Start by facing DW with your weight on the left foot, then step forwards with the right foot, starting to turn towards the right.

■ *Girl LF back*
Start by backing DW with your weight on the right foot, then step back with the left foot, starting to turn towards the right.

move 1

move 2

Move 2 *count 2*

■ *Boy LF side*
Step sideways with the left foot, continuing to turn so you end up backing DC.

■ *Girl RF side*
Step sideways with the right foot, continuing the turn, making sure your right foot is pointing along the LOD.

Move 3 *count 3*

■ *Boy RF closes to LF*

Close the right foot to the left foot, backing LOD.

■ *Girl LF closes to RF*

Close the left foot to the right foot, facing LOD.

move 3

move 4

Move 4 *count 1*

■ *Boy LF back*

Step backwards with your left foot with the intention to turn to the right.

■ *Girl RF forward*

Step forwards with your right foot with the intention to turn to the right.

move 5

move 6

Move 5 *count 2*

■ *Boy RF side*
Step sideways with the right foot.

■ *Girl LF side*
Step sideways with the left foot.

Move 6 *count 3*

■ *Boy LF closes to RF*
Close the left foot to the right foot, facing DC.

■ *Girl RF closes to LF*
Close the right foot to the left foot, backing DC.

You can now continue with the right foot closed change.

> **Note:** Practise this figure until your feet bleed before moving on! I don't mean literally, but you do need to be very comfortable with this figure and be able to do it almost without thinking before you attempt the reverse turn. All good things really do come to those who wait. Patience and practise, practise, practise!

Reverse turn

This is another basic figure that will allow you to get a combination together that you could dance all night.

Point to remember!

Reverse turns always turn to the left, that's anticlockwise. Boys always start on the left foot and girls on the right.

It also consists of six steps and the rhythm goes like this: 1, 2, 3, 1, 2, 3.

Move 1 *count 1*

■ *Boy LF forward*

Start facing DC with your weight on the right foot, then walk forwards with the left foot, starting to turn to the left.

■ *Girl RF back*

Start backing DC with your weight on the left foot, then walk backwards with the right foot, starting to turn to the left.

Move 2 *count 2*

■ *Boy RF side*

Step sideways with the right foot, continuing the turn and backing DW.

■ *Girl LF side*

Step sideways with the left foot, continuing the turn with the foot pointing along the LOD.

Move 3 *count 3*

■ *Boy LF closes to RF*

Close the left foot to the right foot, continuing the turn to end backing LOD.

■ *Girl RF closes to LF*

Close the right foot to the left foot, facing LOD.

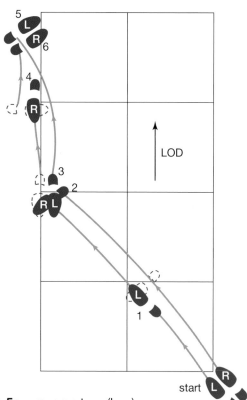

figure 5a   reverse turn (boy)

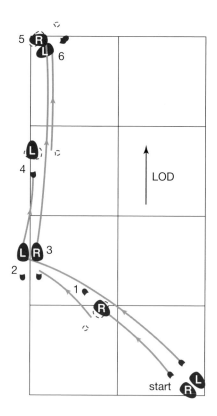

figure 5b   reverse turn (girl)

Move 4 *count 1*

- **Boy RF back**

Step back with the right foot and start to turn left.

- **Girl LF forward**

Step forwards with the left foot and start to turn left.

Move 5 *count 2*

- **Boy LF side**

Step sideways with the left foot but with your body FW.

- **Girl RF side**

Step sideways with the right foot, continuing the turn BW.

Move 6 *count 3*

- **Boy RF closes to LF**

Close the right foot to the left foot, facing DW.

- **Girl LF closes to RF**

Close the left foot to the right foot, backing DW.

You can now continue with the left foot closed change to finish.

Hesitation change

This looks really good and will make you both feel like Fred Astaire and Ginger Rogers. It is also really useful because you can use it as a link between moves 1–3 of the natural turn and moves 1–3 of the reverse turn. It consists of six steps in total and the rhythm goes like this: 1, 2, 3, 1, 2, 3. It starts with steps you already know. Hoorah! The first three steps of the natural turn just to remind you are as follows:

Move 1 *count 1*

- **Boy RF forward**

Start by facing DW with your weight on the left foot, then step forwards with the right foot, starting to turn towards the right.

- **Girl LF back**

Start by backing DW with your weight on the right foot, then step back with the left foot, starting to turn towards the right.

Move 2 *count 2*

- **Boy LF side**

Step sideways with the left foot, continuing to turn so you end up backing DC.

- **Girl RF side**

Step sideways with the right foot, continuing the turn, making sure your right foot is pointing along the LOD.

Move 3 *count 3*

- **Boy RF closes to LF**

Close the right foot to the left foot, backing LOD.

- **Girl LF closes to RF**

Close the left foot to the right foot, facing LOD.

> **Note:** The next three steps are the actual hesitation change.

Move 4 *count 1*

■ *Boy LF back*

Walk back with the left foot and start to turn to the right, backing LOD.

■ *Girl RF forward*

Step forwards with the right foot and start to turn to the right, facing LOD.

Move 5 *count 2*

■ *Boy RF side*

Step sideways with the right foot, continuing the turn, facing DC.

■ *Girl LF side*

Step sideways with the left foot, continuing the turn and backing DC.

Move 6 *count 3 (the cool bit)*

■ *Boy hesitate*

With your weight on the right foot you need to brush your left foot towards your right foot and your body should be facing DC. Keep and hold the weight on the right foot. This creates a small hiatus or what's known as a 'hesitation'.

■ *Girl hesitate*

With your weight on the left foot you need to brush your right foot towards your left foot and your body should be backing DC. Keep and hold the weight on the left foot. This creates a small hiatus or what's known as a 'hesitation'.

You can now carry on with a reverse turn.

Please practise the natural turn into a RF closed change into a reverse turn, finishing with a LF closed change with tracks 4 and 5 on the CD.

> **Note:** It is very important that you don't rush ahead until you have mastered all the moves you have just learnt. And don't forget to try a little rise and fall in there. It would be a good idea to go back to page 26 and remind yourself of the rise and fall action again because it will make a lot more sense now you have more of an idea of the steps.

Outside change

This is a really simple but cool move used as a spacer. It's only three steps and you'll find it useful as a fill-in to extend the basic waltz if the room is bigger than you think and you know you can't fit a whole basic waltz in before the corner. The rhythm goes 1, 2, 3.

Move 1 *count 1*

■ *Boy LF back*

Walk back with the left foot, backing DC.

■ *Girl RF forward*

Walk forwards with the right foot, facing DC.

Move 2 *count 2*

■ *Boy RF back*

Walk back with the right foot, still backing DC.

■ *Girl LF forward*

Walk forwards with the left foot, facing DC.

Move 3 *count 3*

■ *Boy LF side*

Step sideways with the left foot, facing DW.

■ *Girl RF side*

Step sideways with the right foot, backing DW.

You can finish the move by going into a natural turn.

Whisk

This is a great move if there's trouble ahead. For instance, if the couple in front of you have faltered, you wouldn't need to panic and dance directly into them, you could simply go into a whisk, keeping your cool and maintaining your dignity. Floorcraft truly is a wonderful thing.

In 1937, Alex Moore and Pat Kilpatrick (highly respected ballroom dancing gurus) gave what must have been one of the earliest television dance lessons; guess what they were teaching? The whisk! An oldie but a goodie. It was demonstrated on television in order to teach the masses, and it was the newest and hottest thing. Now it is a standard move in the waltz, and a very popular one. Len and Sue will demonstrate and help you get all whisked up into a waltzing frenzy!

This figure consists of a total of seven steps. The first three being the whisk, the last four being your escape from it – the chassé. The rhythm goes: 1, 2, 3, 1, 2, & 3.

Move 1 *count 1*

■ *Boy LF forward*
Start by facing DW with your weight on your right foot, then walk forwards with the left foot.

■ *Girl RF back*
Start by backing DW with your weight on your left foot, then walk backwards with the right foot.

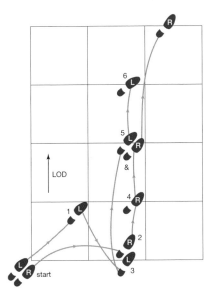

figure 6a   the whisk (boy)

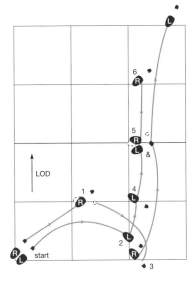

figure 6b   the whisk (girl)

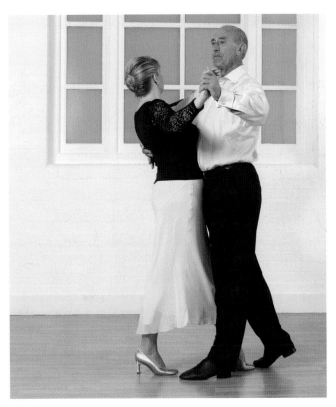

move 1

Move 2 *count 2*

■ *Boy RF side*

Step sideways against the LOD onto the ball of your right foot.

■ *Girl LF side*

Step sideways against the LOD onto the ball of your left foot as you turn to the right, ending facing DC.

move 2

move 3

Move 3 *count 3*

■ *Boy LF behind RF*

Cross your left foot behind your right foot, lowering to the heel.

■ *Girl RF behind LF*

Cross your right foot behind your left foot, lowering to the heel.

Note: You both should now be in the PP (see page 14) and as you can see, Len is entirely happy with that!

The chassé

Here's how you can get out of the whisk in order to carry on!

Move 4 *count 1*

■ *Boy RF forward*

Step forwards with the right foot in PP.

■ *Girl LF forward*

Step forwards with the left foot in PP.

Move 5 *count 2*

■ *Boy LF side*

Step sideways with the left foot with your body facing DW.

■ *Girl RF side*

Step sideways with the right foot with your body FC.

Move 6 *count and*

■ *Boy RF closes to LF*

Close your right foot to your left foot and end with your body facing DW.

■ *Girl LF closes to RF*

Close your left foot to your right foot and ending backing DW.

Move 7 *count 3*

■ *Boy LF side*

Step sideways with the left foot, ending facing DW.

■ *Girl RF side*

Step sideways with your right foot, ending backing DW.

You can follow this figure with a natural turn, however the first step (RF) for the boy will need to be taken outside his partner. Please turn to page 15 for a demonstration by Len and Sue.

Well done for completing the first chapter. Treat yourself by having a nice hot bath then, once you're relaxed, go to the phone and call your local dance school to get class times and dates sorted out for your very first lesson. Do it! You'll never look back. There's a list of schools and organizations in the back of this book (page 196) so no excuses. You have got nothing to lose!

You should now be confident and proficient enough dancing the waltz to be able to get up at any function and not be a total embarrassment to yourself, family or friends. The following amalgamations (a ballroom expression for routine patterns or combos) are only suggestions for you to follow in order to give you an idea of how the steps can actually slot together. You are, of course, free to put your own combos together, and they can be as individual as you are. Go for it!

amalgamations

Amalgamations for the waltz

Routine one
Left foot closed change danced down the LOD
Right foot closed change danced down the LOD
Keep repeating around the room.

Routine two
Left foot closed change
Natural turn
Right foot closed change
Reverse turn
Keep repeating around the room

Routine three
Left foot closed change
Natural turn moves 1–3
Hesitation change
Reverse turn
Whisk and chassé

Make up your own!

....

....

....

....

....

....

....

....

social foxtrot

02 social foxtrot

A little bit of foxy history

Have you ever seen a fox trot? Of course this dance was not, as you may think, an animal based dance but, as one story goes, it was named after a music hall performer who went by the name of Harry Fox. He performed a trotting dance to Ragtime at the Ziegfeld Follies way back in 1914. People loved it and Mr Fox's trot caught on. It was brought from America to the UK in 1915, and was originally quite a wild dance with lots of hops and kicks, until the British got their hands on it, calming it down and making it smoother. Dancing teachers disapproved of all the capers that went with it, and the Imperial Society of Teachers of Dancing in London taught the foxtrot as it is still danced today, in its smooth version. It wasn't standardized until after the First World War, and then became what we now know as a very subtle and flowing English-style dance.

The social foxtrot has an easy, repeatable basic movement, which you'll be able to pick up really quickly, and you will look great dancing this sequence in a matter of minutes.

What music do I dance to?

The beauty and versatility of the foxtrot is that you can dance to a variety of different music, anything with a 2/4 or 4/4 time signature. Just be sure it's not a waltz in 3/4 time as you'll be going against the music, and your steps will feel awkward.

> **Track list**
>
> **6** My introduction – getting you started.
>
> **7** *Have you met Miss Jones?*
>
> **8** *Look what happened to Mabel*

Listen to track 6 of the CD to get a feel for the foxtrot.

Slow Quick Quick

This is just an easy way to remember the timing or rhythm of the dance, and it's also fun to say and relieves the boredom of counting to four. The 'Slow' is held over two beats of the bar, not the pub bar, but the bar of music. The 'Quick' is held for only one beat of the music. The timing, however, can be likened to the pub, in as far as if you were pulling a pint of bitter, that would be slower than the popping of the cork from a Champagne bottle. The rhythm then would be 'pull a pint-pop-pop' representing one slow movement followed by two quick movements. 'Pull-a-pint' is a 'Slow' and the 'pops' are 'Quicks'. Abbreviated it looks like this: SQQ.

- Slow = 2 beats
- Quick = 1 beat
- Quick = 1 beat.

This makes a grand total of four beats to the bar! The tempo that is recommended is set at 32 bars per minute for the slow or social foxtrot.

Now you have your rhythm sorted out, let's talk about the hold.

The hold

The hold should be the same as it is in the waltz (see page 26 for a detailed explanation), and is allowed to be a little less formal. By that I mean just a bit more relaxed. If the dance floor is really heaving with couples, you'll need to make the dance as compact as you can without squeezing each other to death, or breaking your partner's ribcage, gentlemen! The social foxtrot is already a compact dance ideal for these conditions, so keep your steps small. Even if you are terrified, ladies, don't hold on for grim death and dig your nails into your partner's arm as he could retaliate aggressively! Always remember the man is leading the dance, and you have no choice but to go with him. I know it's unfair in this day and age, but it's strictly ballroom!

Note: If you've been naughty and skipped the waltz section (Chapter 1) just to get to the foxtrot and you don't know the hold, go back and have a look at the photos on pages 12 and 13. It would also be a good idea to re-read the section about holds in the waltz chapter (see page 26). Better still, learn the waltz!

Len's top tip

For the foxtrot the first thing to learn
Is the technique for making your turns
So work day and night
Till your movement is right
And soon a dance medal you'll earn

The steps

Basic quarter turns

There are eight steps in the basic foxtrot. Each quarter turn takes up four steps so the first four steps you do will turn you to the right and the next four steps (steps five to eight) will turn you another quarter turn to the left. The rhythm or timing will go like this: Slow Slow Quick Quick Slow Slow Quick Quick. Abbreviated it looks like this: SSQQSSQQ.

Listen to track 6 on the CD where I will talk you slowly through the next eight moves.

Move 1 *count S*
■ *Boy LF forward*
Start by facing DW, with your weight on the right foot, and walk forwards with the left foot.

■ *Girl RF back*
Start by backing DW, with your weight on the left foot, and walk backwards with the right foot.

Move 2 *count S*

■ *Boy RF forward*

Walk forwards with the right foot, starting to turn to the right.

■ *Girl LF back*

Walk backwards with the left foot, starting to turn to the right.

Move 3 *count Q*

■ *Boy LF side FW*

Move your left foot to the side, continuing the turn.

■ *Girl RF side, toe DC*

This is a little tricky for the girl! Move your right foot to the side, continuing the turn, but only a small step otherwise you'll both come apart and potentially fall over. Make sure your toe is pointing DC.

Move 4 *count Q*

■ *Boy RF closes to LF*

As you complete the turn you close your right foot to the left foot. You should end up with your weight on the right foot and backing DC.

■ *Girl LF closes to RF*

As you complete the turn you close your left foot to the right foot with your weight on the left foot, facing DC.

Move 5 *count S*

■ *Boy LF back*

Walk backwards with the left foot.

■ *Girl RF forward*

Walk forwards with the right foot.

Move 6 *count S*

■ *Boy RF back*

Walk backwards with the right foot, starting to turn to the left.

■ *Girl LF forward*

Walk forwards with the left foot, starting to turn to the left.

Move 7 *count Q*

■ *Boy LF side, toe DW*

Move the left foot to the side, taking a small step continuing to turn to the left, and make sure you end up with your toe pointing DW.

■ *Girl RF side*

Move your right foot to the side, continuing to turn to the left, BW.

Move 8 *count Q*

■ *Boy RF closes to LF*

As you complete the turn to the left your right foot closes to the left foot, ending with your weight on the right foot facing DW.

■ *Girl LF closes to RF*

As you complete the turn to the left your left foot closes to the right foot, ending with your weight on the left foot backing DW.

Keep practising these eight steps until you feel comfortable with the steps themselves and the new rhythm, then try it to some music. Why not track 7 of the CD? You can then both keep repeating this basic figure over and over. You will soon want to get on with more exciting combinations, so go on and learn the next step.

Natural pivot turn

The description 'natural' doesn't ever mean that it's going to feel natural or that steps should naturally go in either one direction or another. What it does mean is simply a turn that heads to the right or a clockwise turn. The natural pivot turn is a good move to use around corners, and if you do it three times along the LOD, you will end up right back where you started, backing DC, and you will have completed a full turn. Philip and Lauren will take you through it. Pay special attention to Philip's footwork on move 1.

There are four moves in the natural pivot, the timing of which is: SSQQ.

Move 1 *count S*

■ *Boy LF back*

Start backing DC with your weight on the right foot, then step backwards with a small step (a little to the left) with your left foot, and start turning to the right.

■ *Girl RF forward*

Start facing DC with your weight on the left foot, then step forwards between the boy's feet with your right foot, and start turning to the right.

move 1

move 2

Move 2 *count S*

■ *Boy RF forward*

Transfer your weight forwards onto the right foot, between your girl's feet, as you keep the turn going. You're not actually stepping forwards as such, but just changing weight and turning at the same time. Think of the move as being on the spot.

■ *Girl LF back*

Step backwards on the left (adjusting a little to the left) as you continue to turn to the right.

move 3

move 4

Move 3 *count Q*

■ *Boy LF side*

As you continue to turn to the right, step sideways with your left foot.

■ *Girl RF side*

As you continue to turn to the right, step a *small* step sideways with your right foot.

Move 4 *count Q*

■ *Boy RF closes to LF*

As you are continuing the turn, the right foot closes to the left foot, leaving your weight on the right foot. This creates a slight 'swivel' on the left ball of your foot while you are turning as the right foot closes to the left foot.

■ *Girl LF closes to RF*

As you are continuing the turn, close your left foot to your right foot ending up with your weight on your left foot.

You should now have both managed just over a quarter turn or one-third of a full turn. Do this twice to combat the corner or, as I said earlier, three times if you want to land back in the same position you started in.

Reverse pivot turn

This is a great move for avoiding other couples who are ahead of you on the dance floor, and can also help with coping with the dreaded corners. As with the 'natural' term, the 'reverse' doesn't mean changing gear and reversing backwards, it simply means to turn to the left. It's also done in four moves like the natural pivot turn and the rhythm goes SSQQ.

Move 1 *count S*

■ *Boy LF forward*
Start by facing DW with your weight on the right foot, then step forwards with the left foot forward as you start the turn to the left.

■ *Girl RF back*
Start by backing DW with your weight on the left foot, then step backwards with the right foot as you start the turn to the left.

Move 2 *count S*

■ *Boy RF transfer*
This is a transfer of weight step that feels like a gentle rock. You need to transfer your weight backwards onto the right foot as you continue to turn to the left.

■ *Girl LF transfer*
This is a transfer of weight step that feels like a gentle rock. You need to transfer your weight forwards onto the left foot as you continue to turn to the left.

Move 3 *count Q*

■ *Boy LF side*
As you are turning take a small, sideways step to the left with your toe pointing DC.

■ *Girl RF side*
As you are turning take a sideways step to the right.

Move 4 *count Q*

■ *Boy RF closes to LF*
As your body turns to the left the right foot closes to your left foot, ending with your weight on the right foot, facing DC.

■ *Girl LF closes to RF*
As you turn to the left the left foot closes to your right foot, ending with your weight on the left foot, backing DC.

That's it! If you dance the reverse pivot turn four times, you'll be right back where you started. If you're travelling around a corner, you only have to do it once in order to end up in the right starting position for the new wall. If your objective is to avoid a catastrophe, you'll have to do it several times. Remember that four times brings you back where you started, unlike the natural pivot turn, which takes three times to return to your starting position.

Important point for the boy!
As the boy is leading, he needs to subtly inform his girl of his intentions, otherwise she may think that he will be travelling forwards with the step, and she will not go into the reverse pivot turn, resulting in it all going horribly wrong. To avoid this occurring, the boy shouldn't take his weight too far forward on the first step of LF forward, and he should actually rock gently onto his right foot. Because of this rocking action the boy's left turn must be gentle but deliberate. He must take charge and not be afraid to make decisions! Girls – you may need to exercise your sixth sense when you first try this with a new partner.

Side step

The side step is really useful if you are travelling too far along the room. It holds you up a little or slows down your progression around the dance floor. The side step travels in a sideways movement progressively along the LOD, so that the boy's body is facing the wall and the girl's back is to the wall. You dance it after one basic quarter turn to the right. The side step has four steps and the timing goes like this: SSQQ.

Move 1 *count S*

■ *Boy LF side, RF tap*

After dancing your basic quarter turn, your weight should end up on the right foot, FW. You step sideways with the left foot then, brushing the floor without weight, bring your right foot towards your left foot. Here's the tricky bit – keep your weight on your left foot and just tap the floor with your right foot. Think of it as 'step to the side and tap' or, for short, 'step tap'.

■ *Girl RF side, LF tap*

After dancing your basic quarter turn, your weight should be on the left foot, FC. You step sideways with your right foot then, brushing the floor without weight, bring your left foot towards your right foot. Keep your weight on your right foot and tap the floor with your left foot.

Move 2 *count S*

■ *Boy RF side, LF tap*

Step sideways with the right foot and bring the left foot towards the right foot and tap the left foot.

■ *Girl LF side, RF tap*

Step sideways with the left foot and bring the right foot towards the left foot and tap the right foot.

Move 3 *count Q*

■ *Boy LF side*

Take a small step sideways to the left with the left foot.

■ *Girl RF side*

Take a small step sideways to the right with the right foot.

Move 4 *count Q*

■ *Boy RF closes to LF*

Close your right foot to the left foot, ending with your weight on the right foot.

■ *Girl LF closes to RF*

Close your left foot to the right foot, ending with your weight on the left foot.

You can repeat the side step two or three times and finish with a basic quarter turn to the left. You do need to turn to the right a little on moves 3 and 4 of your last side step in order to get you back on track, ending backing DC and ready to dance a basic quarter turn to the left.

The back corté

The back corté is used when the boy is moving backwards and wants to turn in order to travel in a forward direction. It consists of four steps and the rhythm, which you should now be familiar with, goes like this: SSQQ.

Move 1 *count S*

■ *Boy LF back*
Start by backing DC with your weight on the right foot, then step backwards with the left foot.

■ *Girl RF forward*
Start by facing DC with your weight on the left foot, then step forwards with the right foot.

Move 2 *count S*

■ *Boy RF back*
Step backwards with the right foot.

■ *Girl LF forward*
Step forwards with the left foot.

Move 3 *count Q*

■ *Boy LF side*
Step sideways with the left foot.

■ *Girl RF side*
Step sideways with the right foot.

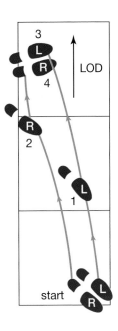
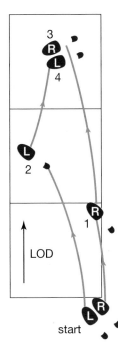

figure 7a
the back corté (boy)

figure 7b
the back corté (girl)

Move 4 *count Q*

■ *Boy RF closes to LF*
Close the right foot to your left foot, with your weight on the right foot, ending facing DW.

■ *Girl LF closes to RF*
Close the left foot to your right foot with your weight on the left foot, ending backing DW.

Promenade walk and chassé

Promenade position (PP)

The PP is not exactly a stroll along the beachfront, but it could be thought of as one because the couple open up to the elements rather than face one another. The term describes the couple moving into a position where the girl's right shoulder and the boy's left shoulder are slightly open, with the girl looking to her right and the boy looking to his left a little more than normal. Both should be looking forward down the LOD. The PP is used often in standard dancing, and you'll be guided when and where to use it as we learn the entry step into PP. You can also turn to the photo on page 51 to see what we are aiming for.

What is a chassé?

A chassé is a series of three consecutive lateral steps, where the feet are closed on the second step. A sliding step in which one foot 'chassés' and displaces the other. The term is French and is pronounced 'shas-say'.

Entry step

This is simply a preparation step to lead you into the PP. It consists of four steps and the rhythm goes SSQQ.

Move 1 *count S*
■ *Boy LF forward*

With your weight on the right foot, facing DW, move your left foot forwards.

■ *Girl RF back*

With your weight on the left foot, backing DW, move your right foot backwards.

Move 2 *count S*
■ *Boy RF forward*

Boys, this is your preparation step so you can masterfully lead your partner into the PP. Walk forwards on the right foot.

■ *Girl LF back*

Get ready girls! Your partner is preparing to lead you into the PP, and you should start to turn to the right, as your left foot is moving backwards.

Move 3 *count Q*
■ *Boy LF side*

Step sideways on the left foot into the PP.

■ *Girl RF side*

Step sideways on the right foot into the PP with your body facing DC.

Move 4 *count Q*
■ *Boy RF closes to LF*

Stay in the PP and close your right foot to the left foot, then place your weight onto the right foot.

■ *Girl LF closes to RF*

Stay in the PP and close your left foot to the right foot, then place your weight onto the left foot.

Now, both go directly into the next step – the promenade walk and chassé.

Promenade walk and chassé

Now you've completed your entry step so magnificently you may now dance beautifully into the promenade walk and chassé which consists of four steps and the rhythm goes like this: SSQQ.

Move 1 *count S*

■ *Boy LF side*

Start as you ended the entry step, facing DW in PP with your weight on the right foot, and take a side step with the left foot, moving along the LOD.

■ *Girl RF side*

Start as you ended the entry step facing DC in PP with your weight on the left foot, and take a side step with the right foot, moving along the LOD.

move 1

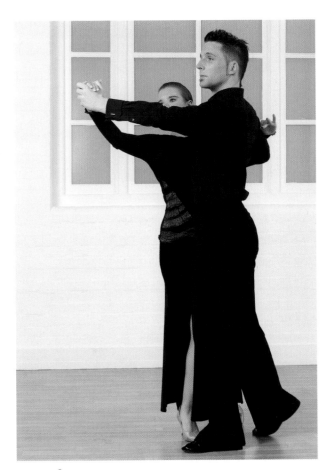

move 2

Move 2 *count S*

■ *Boy RF crosses LF*

Move the right foot forwards in front and across your left foot, remaining in PP.

■ *Girl LF crosses RF*

Move the left foot forwards in front and across your right foot, remaining in PP.

Move 3 *count Q*

■ *Boy LF side*

Take a small step to the side with the left foot, turning to face your partner.

■ *Girl RF side*

Take a small step to the side with the right foot, turning to face your partner.

move 3

move 4

Move 4 *count Q*

■ *Boy RF closes to LF*

Close the right foot to your left foot, changing your weight to the right foot, making sure you are facing DW.

■ *Girl LF closes to RF*

Close the left foot to your right foot, changing your weight to the left foot.

This is a really fun one to do, so feel free to do it repeatedly. You would normally do it two or three times.

Note: The girl needs to turn on the last side and close step to end backing DW, facing her partner in order to dance a basic quarter turn.

Amalgamations for the social foxtrot

You both now have plenty of steps up your sleeves to practise and make perfect, and you can also start running the steps together. There are a number of combinations you will be able to put together yourselves, but here are a few simple combos for you to tackle for starters. Enjoy!

Routine one

Basic quarter turns

Side step

Routine two

Basic quarter turn

Entry step

Promenade walk × 2

Side step

Basic quarter turn

Routine three

Basic quarter turn right (moves 1–4 of basic quarter turn)

Back corté

Reverse pivot turns × 3

Basic quarter turn left (moves 5–8 of basic quarter turn)

make up your own

Make up your own!

....

....

....

....

....

....

....

quickstep

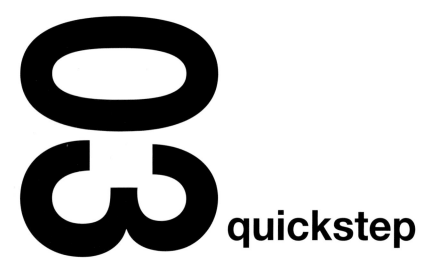

03 quickstep

A quick little bit of step history

I really love this particular dance because it is lively, bouncy, vibrant and full of energy! I hope it will be one of your favourites for the very same reasons. The quickstep has a mixed background as it has developed over the years with many different influences. I suppose you could say that when the one-step and rag gradually died a death, people wanted to replace it with something, and during the early 1920s when life and popular music were getting faster, dancers had to speed up the foxtrot to accommodate the music – the quick foxtrot was born.

Meanwhile, as the social or slow foxtrot was getting slower and smoother, another explosion of dance was to hit the scene and that was the Charleston. The Charleston comes from the town of Charleston in South Carolina, USA, where black dockworkers danced to amuse themselves. It then transported itself to New York where it became a hit in the Ziegfeld Follies of 1923. Its side kicking steps were soon adopted by the flappers and their partners. The Charleston was the trendiest dance of 1925 and caused a sensation! The world went crazy and danced in the streets, stopping traffic. It was exciting, high kicking, demented, electrifying, terrifying, and it was regarded as a danger to public health because of the potential injuries or strain it could cause to your knees, ankles and heart, not to mention the extreme dangers to others on the dance floor. There used to be notices put up saying 'P.C.Q.', which stands for 'Please Charleston Quietly', and also signs saying 'No Kicking Please'.

The Charleston didn't enjoy a long life, and was more of a fad of the time, but it did leave behind a remarkable legacy. It came to symbolize the jazz age, and remains one of the most enduring images of the 1920s. When the Charleston eventually died its certain death in 1927, it was combined with the quick foxtrot to become the new 'quick time foxtrot and Charleston' This was a bit of a mouthful, so the name was changed to the quickstep. The quickstep is full of body swing movements and syncopated hops at major speeds, which is exactly why you are going to love it!

What music do I dance to?

The time signature of the quickstep is 4/4. That's four beats to each bar of music. As with the foxtrot, you count with quicks and slows, and you should now be familiar with this concept. However, the speed is much faster than the foxtrot, which glides along at 32 bars per minute, whereas the quickstep rockets along at a whopping 50 bars per minute! It's good to dance the quickstep at speeds of anywhere between 48–52 bars per minute. As it's a fast dance, you'll need to get up to speed to enjoy the quickstep fully, so practise it really slowly until you become completely familiar and confident with it. Gradually increase the tempo at your own pace and you and your partner will both be flying around that dance floor. A great tip is to take smaller steps, which will help you control your body and help you to cope with the tempo.

Track list

9 My introduction – getting you started.

10 *Dancin' Fool*

11 *Don't Tell Mama*

Go to the CD and put on track **9**.

Heel leads

When I use the word 'walk', this is technically known as a 'heel lead'. Which simply means first putting your heel down before the ball of your foot. A 'heel' step is taken first with the heel in contact with the floor, and then with the whole foot flat. There are some new terms that you need to familiarize yourself with for this dance:

- **heel lead to ball of foot** – the heel is placed down in contact with the floor before rising to the ball of the foot.
- **heel lead to whole foot** – the heel is placed down in contact with the floor followed by the whole foot flat on the floor.
- **ball of foot to heel** – after rising to the ball of the foot, the heel is lowered to the floor with the weight on the whole foot.
- **heel-pivot** – after the whole foot is placed in contact with the floor and the toe is lifted leaving the weight on the heel, a turn or 'pivot' on the heel of that foot can then be achieved.

The hold

Easy! The hold for the quickstep is the same as for the waltz. On pages 12 and 13 there are photos of it to remind you but, if you've been a diligent student, you'll know it off the top of your head!

Len's top tip

In the quickstep you are moving at speed
So ladies follow his lead
You will fly round the floor
At 50 or more
So safety belts are the things that you need!

Note: I have chosen to mention footwork in the quickstep chapter in order to give you a little more insight into the intricacies of ballroom dancing – plus it will help you to move at the required speed of this particular dance.

The steps

Basic quickstep progressive chassé

This is a basic pattern for the quickstep. I have used an amalgamation of part of a quarter turn as an entry step and the progressive chassé. It may all seem like a foreign language at the moment, but it sounds more complicated than it actually is. Take your time and learn this thoroughly.

There are ten moves to learn and the rhythm goes like this: SSQQSSQQSS.

Please listen to track 9 where I will talk you through this fierce basic figure.

Move 1 *count S*

■ *Boy LF forward*

Start by facing DW with your weight on your right foot, then step forwards with the left foot.

■ *Girl RF back*

Start by backing DW with your weight on your left foot, then step backwards with the right foot.

Move 2 *count S*

■ *Boy RF forward*

Step forwards with the right foot and start turning to the right.

■ *Girl LF back*

Step backwards with the left foot and start turning to the right.

move 1

move 2

Move 3 *count Q*

■ *Boy LF side*

Take a step sideways with the left foot as you continue to turn to the right.

■ *Girl RF side*

Take a step sideways with the right foot as you continue to turn to the right.

move 3

move 4

Move 4 *count Q*

■ *Boy RF closes to LF*

Close your right foot to the left foot.

■ *Girl LF closes to RF*

Close your left foot to the right foot.

Move 5 *count S*

■ *Boy LF side*

Take a step sideways with the left foot with your body now backing DC.

■ *Girl RF side*

Take a step sideways with the right foot with your body facing DC.

move 5

move 6

Move 6 *count S*

■ *Boy RF back*

Step backwards with the right foot, ball of foot to heel as you start turning to the left.

■ *Girl LF forward*

Step forwards with the left foot, heel lead to the ball of foot as you start turning to the left.

Move 7 *count Q*

■ *Boy LF side*

Step sideways onto the ball of your left foot, pointing the left foot DW with your body FW.

■ *Girl RF side*

Step sideways onto the ball of your right foot, turning a little to the left, making sure that your body is backing the wall.

move 7

move 8

Move 8 *count Q*

■ *Boy RF closes to LF*

Up on both balls now, close your right foot to the left foot with your body and feet facing DW. Your body should have to turn ever so slightly to the left.

■ *Girl LF closes to RF*

As you continue the turn on the ball of your right foot, close the ball of the left foot to the right foot. Your body and feet will be backing DW with your weight on the left foot.

move 9

move 10

Move 9 *count S*

■ *Boy LF side*

Move your left foot sideways and just a little bit forwards as you are now in the preparation mode to step outside your partner. You are about to lower ball to heel as the following step (move 10) is taken.

■ *Girl RF side*

Move your right foot sideways, backing DW, ending up with your right foot to the side but just a little back compared to your left foot. You are about to lower ball to heel as the following step (move 10) is taken.

Move 10 *count S*

This is a move that gets you out of the progressive chassé so you can continue with other steps, and it's the first time the boy will have stepped outside the girl in the quickstep – see the close-up photograph on the opposite page which demonstrates this perfectly or turn to page 15 to see Len and Sue do it.

■ *Boy RF forward*

Walk forwards on your right foot outside your partner (OP) with your body facing DW. This is a heel lead to the whole of the foot.

■ *Girl LF back*

With your partner on the outside of you, walk backwards on the left foot with your body backing DW.

Congratulations! You've just done a quickstep! You can both now keep repeating this from move 3–10 all the way around the room or continue with the next fabulous step, and this is the formidable lock step, from move 2 onwards.

close-up of move 10

The lock step

The lock step is the name in ballroom dancing for the feet crossing loosely and not actually locking. Now you've mastered the basic quickstep, the time has come to be the proud owners of the lock! Naturally, as the boy dances the forward lock, the girl will dance the backward lock.

You can use this figure to progress your way around the dance floor or just because you feel like it!

Lock step

Impress yourself and your friends with this step. It can be danced in a forward direction or a backward direction. There are five moves and the rhythm goes like this: SQQSS.

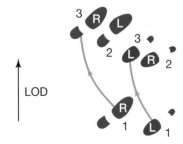

figure 8   lock step

Move 1 *count S*

■ *Boy RF forward*

Start facing DW with your weight on the left foot then walk forwards with the right foot outside your girl. This is a heel lead and you're about to rise up onto the ball of your right foot.

■ *Girl LF back*

Start by backing DW with your weight on the right foot, then walk backwards on the ball of your left foot, keeping your partner on your right side. Lower the heel of the left foot.

move 1

move 2

Move 2 *count Q*

■ *Boy LF diagonally forward*

On the ball of the right foot, step diagonally forwards with your left foot.

■ *Girl RF back*

Step backwards onto the ball of your right foot.

Move 3 *count Q*

■ *Boy RF crosses behind LF*

On the balls of your feet, cross your right foot behind your left foot, putting your weight onto the ball of the right foot.

■ *Girl LF crosses front RF*

On the balls of your feet, cross your left foot in front of your right foot, putting your weight onto the ball of the left foot.

Move 4 (below) *count S*

■ *Boy LF diagonally forward*

As you travel DW your left foot is going to take a diagonal step forward onto the ball of the foot then lower to the heel as the next step (move 5) is taken.

move 3

■ *Girl RF diagonally back*

Move your right foot diagonally backwards on the ball of that foot, then lower to the heel as the next step (move 5) is taken.

Move 5 *count S*

■ *Boy RF forward*

Walk forwards on your right foot outside your partner (OP) with your body facing DW. This is a heel lead to the whole of the foot.

■ *Girl LF back*

Step backwards with your left foot.

You may have noticed that move 5 and move 1 are the same. These steps get you in and out of the lock step. You will also notice that move 10 of the progressive chassé finishes with move 1 of the forward lock step, marrying or knitting the steps together.

move 4

The natural turn with hesitation

You should be well acquainted with this step from the natural turn in the waltz. The natural turn in the quickstep is similar but has different timing. As in the foxtrot and the quickstep, we count in quicks and slows so the timing or rhythm for the natural turn in the quickstep time should be: SQQSSS.

It consists of six moves and is one of the most useful moves to use at the corners.

Move 1 *count S*

■ *Boy RF forward*

Start facing DW with your weight on the left foot, then walk forwards with the right foot and start to turn to the right.

> **Note:** As move 2 with the left foot goes into position, you are going to rise from heel lead to ball.

■ *Girl LF back*

Start backing DW with your weight on the right foot, then walk backwards with the left foot and start to turn to the right. Lower the ball of foot to heel.

Move 2 *count Q*

■ *Boy LF side*

As you continue the turn, move sideways onto the ball of your left foot, backing DC.

■ *Girl RF side*

As you continue the turn, move sideways onto the ball of your right foot, pointing to the LOD.

Move 3 *count Q*

■ *Boy RF closes to LF*

Continue turning on the ball of the left foot and close your right foot to your left foot, lowering the right heel as Move 4 is taken. Make sure your weight is on the right foot backing LOD.

■ *Girl LF closes to RF*

Continuing to turn your body, close the left foot to your right foot, lowering the left heel as move 4 is taken. Your body should be facing LOD with the weight on the left foot.

Move 4 *count S*

■ *Boy LF back*

Move the left foot backwards, turning your body to the right, as you turn to the right on the left heel.

■ *Girl RF forward*

Move the right foot forwards, turning your body to the right, as you turn to the right on the ball of your right foot, move 5 is taken.

Move 5 *count S*

■ *Boy RF side*

Bring your right foot back and place it to the side of your left foot, placing your weight on the whole of the right foot.

■ *Girl LF side*

Step sideways with your left foot, placing your weight on the ball of your left foot.

Move 6 *count S*

■ *Boy drag LF to RF hesitate*

With your weight on the whole of the right foot release your left heel and drag your left foot to your right foot, hesitate and end facing DC.

■ *Girl drag RF to LF hesitate*

At the same time that you're dragging your right foot towards your left foot, without any weight, lower your left heel. Hesitate and end backing DC.

The chassé reverse turn with a chassé ending

The chassé reverse turn consists of seven steps and the rhythm goes like this: SQQSQQS.

Move 1 *count S*

■ *Boy LF forward*

Start with your weight on the right foot, facing DC, then walk forwards with the left foot, starting to turn to the left. You move from a heel lead to the ball of foot as move 2 gets into position.

■ *Girl RF back*

Start with your weight on the left foot, backing DC, then walk backwards with the right foot as you start the turn to the left with the ball of foot lowering to heel.

Move 2 *count Q*

■ *Boy RF side*

As you continue the turn and back DW move your right foot sideways, on the ball of the foot.

■ *Girl LF side*

As you continue the turn move your left foot sideways, on the ball of the foot and pointing it to the LOD.

Move 3 *count Q*

■ *Boy LF closes to RF*

The turn continues on the ball of the right foot as you close the left foot to your right foot. Your body is backing LOD with your weight on the left foot.

> **Note:** The ball of your left foot lowers to the heel as move 4 is taken.

■ *Girl RF closes to LF*

Continue turning the body and close the right foot to your left foot, ending up facing LOD with your weight on the right foot.

> **Note:** The ball of your right foot lowers to the heel as move 4 is taken.

Move 4 *count S*

■ *Boy RF back*

Step back along the LOD with the right foot as you start to turn to the left.

■ *Girl LF forward*

Step forwards with the left foot as you start to turn to the left, heel lead to the ball of foot.

Move 5 *count Q*

■ *Boy LF side*

Take a step sideways with the left foot, still turning.

■ *Girl RF side*

You are still on the turn as you take a small step to the side on the ball of the foot, BW.

Move 6 *count Q*

■ *Boy RF closes to LF*

As you continue the turn close your right foot to the left foot, placing your weight on the whole of the right foot with your body facing DW.

■ *Girl LF closes to RF*

Still turning on the right foot close your left foot to the right foot, ending up with your weight on the left foot and backing DW.

> **Note:** Lower your left heel as you start move 7.

Move 7 *count S*

■ *Boy LF forward*

Step sideways and slightly forwards with your left foot, facing DW.

■ *Girl RF back*

Step sideways and slightly backwards with your right foot backing DW.

The natural pivot turn at a corner

The natural pivot turn is a fantastic and extremely useful step to use at a corner. It's a hard one to master for beginners, but the boys might find it easier to lead than the natural turn. See how you go! With experience, you can also use it to travel along the sides of the room if you need to catch up with your friends. You can put a basic quickstep before this move. It consists of four steps and the rhythm goes like this: SQQS.

Move 1 *count S*

■ *Boy RF forward*

Start by facing DW near a corner of the room, with your weight on the left foot, then walk (heel lead) forwards and OP with the right foot, starting to turn to the right.

■ *Girl LF back*

Start by backing DW near a corner of the room, with your weight on the right foot then step backwards with the left foot (ball to heel).

Move 2 *count Q*

■ *Boy LF side*

Step sideways on the ball of the left foot as you continue to turn and back DC.

■ *Girl RF side*

Step sideways on the ball of the right foot and continue the turn, pointing your toe to the LOD.

Move 3 *count Q*

■ *Boy RF closes to LF*

Turning on the ball of the left foot to the right, close the right foot to your left foot, up on both balls now, putting your weight on the right foot and body backing the LOD.

> **Note:** You're going to lower the right heel as move 4 is taken.

■ *Girl LF closes to RF*

As the turn continues, close the left foot to the right foot, ending up facing the LOD with your weight on the left foot.

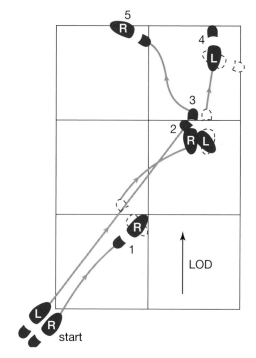

figure 9a   the natural pivot turn (boy)

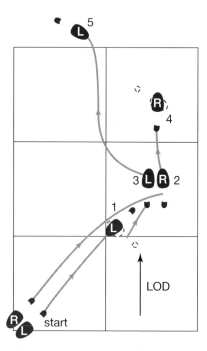

figure 9b   the natural pivot turn (girl)

Note: You're going to lower the left heel as move 4 is taken.

Move 4 *count S*

■ *Boy LF back then RF forward*

Step backwards onto the ball of your left foot, just slightly to the left, then turn to the right on the ball of your left foot, just letting the right heel touch the floor (think of it as drawing a semi-circle on the floor with your heel). Hold your right foot forwards in line with your left foot during the turn, then release the heel of your left foot ending with your weight on the ball of your left foot. Your body should now be facing DW of the new wall.

Note: To continue dancing along the new wall and LOD you need to walk forwards on your right foot, making this step the second step of the basic quarter turns (see move 5 or page 70).

■ *Girl RF forward LF back*

On a heel lead, step forwards onto the right foot, facing the LOD, then turn on the ball of that foot to the right. Allow your left foot to trail behind you as you turn. Your body should end up backing DW of the new wall.

Note: To continue dancing along the new wall and LOD you need to take the weight back on to the left foot, making this the second step of the basic quarter turns.

Zig zag

The zig zag is a popular step in the quickstep because it looks great, and feels great to dance! There are five steps in this figure and the rhythm goes like this: SSSSS. You can precede this with the natural turn with hesitation.

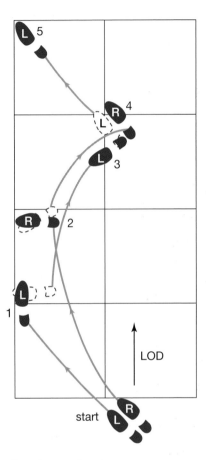

figure 10a   the zig zag (boy)

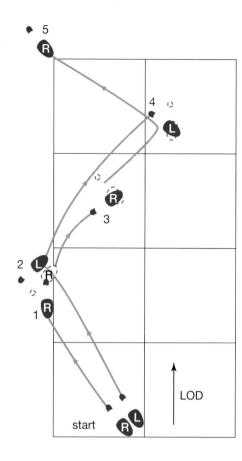

figure 10b   the zig zag (girl)

Move 1 *count S*

■ *Boy LF forward*

Start by facing DC, then step (heel lead to ball) forwards with your left foot, turning your body to the left.

■ *Girl RF back*

Start by backing DC, then step (ball to heel) backwards with the right foot, turning your body to the left.

Move 2 *count S*

■ *Boy RF side*

Take a sideways step (ball to heel) onto the right foot FC along the LOD.

■ *Girl LF closes to RF heel turn*

Close your left foot to your right foot, turning on your right heel, then finish with your weight on the left foot facing DW.

Move 3 *count S*

■ *Boy LF back*

Continue turning a little to the left and step back on your left foot, keeping your partner on the outside, then start to turn your body to the right, backing DW.

■ *Girl RF forward*

Take your right foot forwards across the body, facing DW and OP, then begin to turn to the right.

Move 4 *count S*

■ *Boy RF back to LF*

Bring your right foot back to your left foot, and at the same time you should be turning to the right on your left heel (heel turn). End up with the weight on your right foot and your body facing DC.

■ *Girl LF side*

Step sideways across the LOD with the left foot with your body backing DC.

Move 5 *count S*

■ *Boy LF forward*

Walk forwards with your left foot (whole foot), facing DC.

■ *Girl RF back*

Close the right foot to your left foot and then step backwards with your right foot (ball) backing DC.

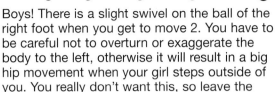

Warning! Danger! Danger! Danger!

Boys! There is a slight swivel on the ball of the right foot when you get to move 2. You have to be careful not to overturn or exaggerate the body to the left, otherwise it will result in a big hip movement when your girl steps outside of you. You really don't want this, so leave the hot hip action for the rumba!

Note: To exit the zig zag the boy steps forwards with his left foot, outside the girl (OP), and continues with the chassé reverse turn with a chassé ending. The girl steps back with her right foot and continues with the chassé reverse turn with a chassé ending.

With the basics you've just learnt, you can now have a go at the following combos!

amalgamations

Amalgamations for the quickstep
Routine one
Basic quickstep with progressive chassé

Lock step

Basic quickstep

Routine two
Basic quickstep with progressive chassé

Lock step

Natural turn with hesitation

Chassé reverse turn

Basic quickstep

Routine three
Natural pivot turn

Lock step

Natural turn with hesitation

Zig zag

Chassé reverse turn

Lock step

Note: All of these combos can be repeated around the room over and over!

Make up your own!

....

....

....

....

....

....

....

tango

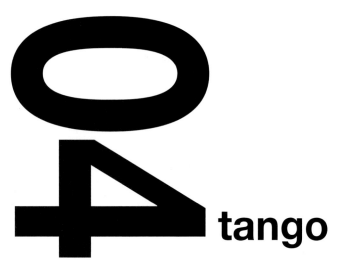

04 tango

A little bit of erotic history

I have used the tango in just about every show I have ever choreographed. This is not just because I think it's an amazingly passionate, erotic and sensual dance, but also because it tells a story. Tango is full of drama, and in the theatre you can't get enough of that. The dance has a wicked history too and has developed considerably over the years. It is said to be a mixture of the Tangano, which was a dance associated with the African slaves that were transported to Haiti and Cuba in the eighteenth century, and the Habañera, a Cuban dance of the nineteenth century. The tango was a very erotic dance that became popular in the poor, lower-class ghettos *Barria de Las Ranas* on the outskirts of Buenos Aires in the late nineteenth century. The city back then was filled with immigrants and transients from Europe and Africa. Mostly they were lonely and looking for companionship in their new foreign habitat. Tango became associated with violence, pimps and prostitutes, and was shunned by the upper levels of polite Buenos Aires society. Story-wise, the tango began as a pantomime of communication between the prostitute and pimp, improvised and full of emotional outpouring and suggestive gyration.

There are, of course, many stories about the tango but the following one is a particular favourite of mine, and may give a clue to how the style of the tango came about. The gauchos or cowboys of Argentina wore chaps that hardened from the foam and sweat of the horses' body. Like all good cowboys, the gauchos walked with the knees flexed and were always hungry for women. They would rock up to the crowded night clubs and ask the prostitutes to dance. Since the gauchos hadn't showered for a while, the lady would dance in the crook of the man's right arm, holding her head back. Her right hand was held low on his left hip, close to his pocket looking for a payment for dancing with him. The man danced in a curving fashion because the floor was generally small with round tables, and he danced around and between them.

In the early 1900s, a less vulgar form of tango was exported to France, where it was further refined and quickly gained popularity with the Parisian high society, adding classy clothes, ballrooms, lyrics, and a 'tango orchestra'. It arrived in England in 1912 after people had seen it performed at the fashionable casino ballrooms of Deauville and Dinard. Demand for the dance was high, and the tango was revolutionized for the rich and became popular all over Europe, the USA, and came full circle when it was danced in its new acceptable guise by the bourgeoisie of Argentina.

Thés Tango, or in English 'tango teas', were the thing to do in London and Paris. They were held in the late afternoons and early evenings. The restless and fashionable could go and tango between tea tables to live music. The Savoy Hotel in London was one of the first places to entertain the idea, and it caught on like wildfire.

When the First World War was declared in 1914 the tango lost its verve, but in the 1920s it had a second wind as the 'New French tango'. It was this version that Rudolf Valentino made famous in the 1921 film *The Four*

Horsemen of the Apocalypse. The tango had become a lot more exotic and spicy.

The modern tango you are about to learn bears little resemblance to the original or the tango that Valentino danced. It's now a staccato dance without the licentious and lascivious qualities due to the standards laid down by the Committee of the Imperial Society of Teachers of Dancing who met in London in the 1920s to bring order out of chaos.

The tango's golden age was the 1940s, but it came back into the public eye in the 1980s, due mainly to the success of the stage show *Tango Argentina*. You can see Al Pacino dance the tango in the film *Scent of a Woman* or Madonna in the movie *Evita*, and Caroline O'Conner in Baz Luhrmann's film *Moulin Rouge*.

There are three predominant styles of tango:

1 **Show tango** is the style most people have seen as it's used in film and stage shows.
2 **Tango de salon** is for ballrooms and is more formal.
3 **Tango orillero** is for small spaces, like tango cafés and bars. It has lots of weaving patterns that are accomplished in very little space.

What music do I dance to?

The time signature for the tango is 2/4, which means that there are two beats to every bar of music. Both of the beats have an accent – a definite downbeat on beats 1 and 2. There are other hidden beats between beats 1 and 2 that are called 'half beats'. We call it an 'and' count like this: 1 and 2 and 1 and 2 and, etc.

In the tango, just like the foxtrot and quickstep, we also use our Slows and Quicks, which you are extremely familiar with now. This is how they work rhythm-wise for the tango:

● Slow = 1 beat
● Quick = ¹/₂ beat (the 'and' count).

The tempo should be set at approximately 33 bars to the minute.

Track list

12 My introduction – getting you started.

13 *Tres Hombres Paraglidos*

14 *Whatever Lola Wants*

Why don't you listen to track **12** on the CD to get you in the mood? You'll immediately discover why the tango is so popular and I challenge you to not want to take to the floor immediately.

The hold

This hold is up close and very personal! The man is dominant, which creates the need for a closer hold than in the waltz. The tango is more compact than any of the other moving dances. The boy places his right arm further around the girl, and closes his left forearm a little more inwards. You should both notice that the girl is now being held slightly more to the boy's right side. Because you've both moved in closer, the girl's left arm and hand will be further around the boy and a little lower than in the waltz. Her left hand should then be placed under the boy's left shoulder blade with the fingers held together and the palm facing downwards. Ladies, you will notice your right forearm will be drawn inwards as a result of the boy moving his left arm in slightly.

The walk

All walking steps in the tango are picked up a little from the floor and placed into position, as opposed to other dances which we endeavour to keep really smooth and make glide across the dance floor. The knees are kept slightly relaxed, and the muscles of the legs are tensed so your body doesn't move up and down as you take your weight from one step to the other. Think of it as walking on one level and as if you have a book on your head. We don't want rise and fall. The next little section can be practised by both of you at the same time because it's the same for the boy as it is for the girl.

Forward walk

Count slow (1 and)

To begin, stand in the tango hold (turn to page 14 and you will see Sue and I demonstrate the tango front view) with your feet together. Here's the important bit – slide your right foot back until your toe is level with the arch of your left foot. This puts you in a position that will keep your knees flexed (bent) slightly and will also stop your knees bashing each other. Now, have your weight on the right foot, then just as in a normal walk take your left foot forwards, heel first then the whole of the foot. Let the heel of your back foot, the right foot, release but keep some weight on the ball of that right foot. Almost all of your body weight should now be over your left foot with a little weight on the ball of the right.

Count slow (2 and)

As you transfer your weight completely onto the left foot, your right foot is going to move towards your left foot by skimming the floor and, as it arrives, you need to lift it and take it forwards, heel first then the whole foot.

Backward walk

Count slow (1 and)

Stand in the tango hold as above, but this time slide your left foot forwards until your heel is level with the arch of your right foot, and again knees flexed. With the weight on the left foot, take your right foot back onto the ball of the foot then release the toe of the left foot, maintaining some weight on the heel. Your weight should be travelling to the right foot.

Count slow (2 and)

As you transfer your weight completely over the right foot lift the left foot and place it sharply back at the same time releasing the toe of the right foot. You should notice that the right heel lowers just prior to the left foot passing it, as the left foot goes into the next back walk.

> **Note:** As a general rule, in the tango the man **always** starts with his left foot; the lady **always** starts with her right foot!

(turn to page 14

Len's top tip

Staccato is the key to the tango
Hold tight girls, and just feel the man go
Down Argentine way
They dance it all day
But never, of course to a banjo.

The steps

Rock turn

There are eight steps and the rhythm of this sequence goes like this: SSQQSQQS.

Please play track **12** of the CD to hear me guide you through this fab figure.

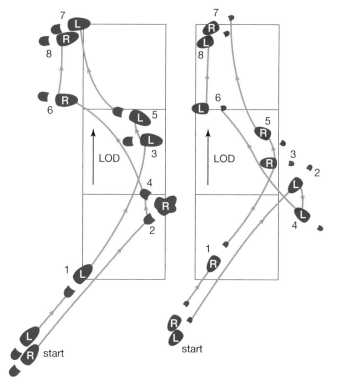

figure 11a the rock turn (boy)

figure 11b the rock turn (girl)

Move 1 *count S*

■ *Boy LF forward*
Start facing DW with your weight on the right foot then walk forwards with the left foot.

■ *Girl RF back*
Start by backing DW with your weight on the left foot, then walk backwards with the right foot.

move 1

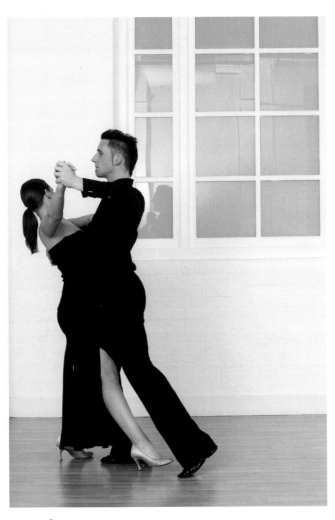

move 2

Move 2 *count S*

■ *Boy RF forward*
Walk forwards with your right foot and start to turn to the right.

■ *Girl LF back*
Walk backwards with your left foot and start to turn to the right.

Move 3 *count Q*

■ *Boy LF side*

Move your left foot sideways and a little backwards, your body is BC.

■ *Girl RF between*

This step has a powerful potential if misused. Careful ladies and go easy!

Move your right foot a little to the right between the boy's feet and place your weight on it.

move 3

move 4

Move 4 *count Q*

■ *Boy RF transfer*

Transfer your weight forwards onto your right foot between the girl's feet.

■ *Girl LF left*

Move your left foot a little to the left, placing the weight on it.

Move 5 *count S*

■ *Boy LF back*

Only take a tiny step backwards with the left foot.

■ *Girl RF forward*

Take a tiny step forwards with the right foot.

move 5

move 6

Move 6 *count Q*

■ *Boy RF back*

Step backwards with your right foot to the centre, turning a little to the left.

■ *Girl LF forward*

Step forwards with your left foot to the centre, also turning to the left.

move 7

move 8

Move 7 *count Q*

■ *Boy LF side*
Step sideways with the left foot with your left toe turned a little to the left and your body FW.

■ *Girl RF side*
Step sideways and slightly back with the right foot, as you continue the turn.

Move 8 *count S*

■ *Boy RF closes to LF*
As your body is turning to the left close your right foot (slightly backwards) to the left foot. Your weight should now be on the right foot and you should be facing DW.

■ *Girl LF closes to RF*
As your body continues the turn you need to close your left foot (slightly forwards) to the right foot. Your weight should now be on your left foot and you should be backing DW.

You can now just keep repeating this section over and over. If you get bored, re-read 'the walk' section to make sure you have understood it fully. Then put all the points into practice and have some fun! When you feel ready, go on to the basic reverse turn.

Basic reverse turn

You will find the basic reverse turn easy to dance but some beginners have a little trouble leading it. With practice you'll be fierce! There are six steps and the rhythm for this is: QQSQQS.

Move 1 *count Q*

■ **Boy LF forward**

Start facing DC with your weight on your right foot then walk forwards with the left foot and start to turn to the left.

■ **Girl RF back**

Start by backing DC with your weight on your left foot, then walk backwards with the right foot and start to turn left.

Move 2 *count Q*

■ **Boy RF side**

Step to the side and slightly back with your right foot as you continue the turn, body backing the LOD.

■ **Girl LF side**

Step to the side and slightly forward with your left foot, making sure your toe is pointing down the LOD.

Move 3 *count S*

■ **Boy LF crosses front RF**

Still turning, cross your left foot in front of your right foot, taking your weight onto the left foot with your body backing the LOD.

■ **Girl RF closes to LF**

As you continue the turn your right foot will close to your left foot, slightly back, ending up with your weight on the right foot, body facing the LOD.

Move 4 *count Q*

■ **Boy RF back**

Step backwards with the right foot as you start to turn to the left.

■ **Girl LF forward**

Walk forwards with the left foot as you start to turn to the left.

Move 5 *count Q*

■ **Boy LF side**

As you continue the turn, step sideways with your left foot, making sure your left toe is turned a little to the left and your body is FW.

■ **Girl RF side**

As you continue the turn, step to the side and slightly backwards with the right foot, backing DW.

Move 6 *count S*

■ **Boy RF closes to LF**

Close your right foot (slightly backwards) to your left foot as your body continues turning to the left. Your weight should now be on the right foot with your body facing DW.

■ **Girl LF closes to RF**

Close your left foot (slightly forwards) to your right foot as your body continues turning left. Your weight should end up on the left foot and body end backing DW.

> **Note:** In order to dance a rock turn into a basic reverse turn you need to overturn the last three moves of the rock turn to end with the boy facing DC and the girl backing DC. This also applies to the open reverse turn overleaf. To find out more about overturn and how you achieve it, turn to page 91.

Open reverse turn closed finish

This is a really easy figure to learn because it's just like the reverse turns in the quickstep and foxtrot! It consists of six steps and the rhythm goes like this: QQSQQS.

Move 1 *count Q*

■ *Boy LF forward*

Start facing DC with your weight on your right foot, then walk forwards with the left foot as you start the turn to the left.

■ *Girl RF back*

Start by backing DC with your weight on your left foot, then walk backwards with the right foot as you start the turn to the left.

Move 2 *count Q*

■ *Boy RF side*

Step to the side and slightly back with the right foot as you continue to turn, body backing the LOD.

■ *Girl LF closes to RF*

Your left foot closes to your right foot as you continue to turn, noting your left foot pointing down the LOD, and releasing the right heel.

Move 3 *count S*

■ *Boy LF back*

Step backwards with your left foot, backing the LOD.

■ *Girl RF forward*

Walk forwards with your right foot, body facing the LOD.

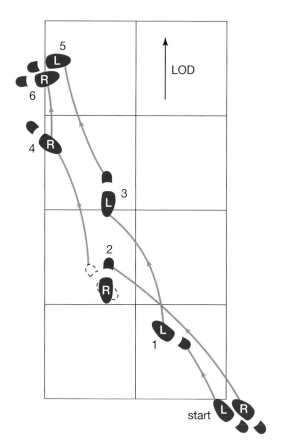

figure 12a the open reverse turn (boy)

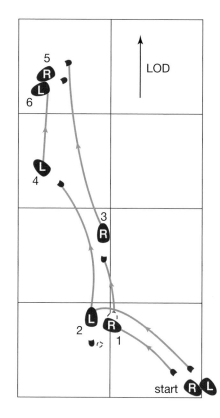

figure 12b the open reverse turn (girl)

Move 4 count Q

■ *Boy RF back*

Step backwards with the right foot, starting to turn to the left.

■ *Girl LF forward*

Walk forwards with the left foot, starting to turn to the left.

Move 5 count Q

■ *Boy LF side*

This is all about the left! As you continue to turn to the left you step sideways to the left with your left toe pointing a little leftwards.

■ *Girl RF side*

As you continue the turn step to the side and slightly back with the right foot, body backing DW.

Move 6 count S

■ *Boy RF closes to LF*

Turning your body to the left, close your right foot (slightly backwards) to the left foot, placing your weight on to the right foot with your body facing DW.

> **Note:** This can be followed by a walk forwards on the left.

■ *Girl LF closes to RF*

Close your left foot (slightly forwards), to your right foot with your weight ending on the left foot and body backing DW.

> **Note:** This can be followed by a walk backwards on the right foot.

Back corté

The back corté is a figure used if the boy is travelling backwards to the LOD and wants to go in a forward direction. It consists of four moves and the rhythm used is: SQQS.

Move 1 count S

■ *Boy LF back*

Start in the normal tango hold with your body backing the LOD and your weight on the right foot, then walk backwards with your left foot.

■ *Girl RF forward*

Start with your weight on the left foot and body facing the LOD, then walk forwards with your right foot.

move 1

Move 2 *count Q*

■ *Boy RF back*

Walk backwards with your right foot, starting to turn to the left.

■ *Girl LF forward*

Walk forwards with your left foot, starting to turn to the left.

move 2

move 3

Move 3 *count Q*

■ *Boy LF side*

As you continue the turn, step sideways with your left foot with your left toe pointing a little to the left, and body FW.

■ *Girl RF side*

As you continue the turn, step a little back but sideways with your right foot, backing DW.

Move 4 *count S*

■ *Boy RF closes to LF*
Your body is still turning left as you close your right foot (slightly back) to the left foot. Your weight should now be on your right foot, ending with your body facing DW.

■ *Girl LF closes to RF*
Your body is still turning left as you close your left foot (slightly forwards) to the right foot. Your weight should now be on your left foot, ending with your body backing DW.

move 4

Note: You can both now follow this sequence with a walk forwards on your free foot. For the boy it will be the **left** foot and the girl the **right** foot. The back corté can be followed with a link (see below), a left foot rock or any reverse turn.

Link into closed promenade

In PP, the boy's right side and the girl's left side are kept close together. In direct opposition to that, in order to make the body appear in a V-shape, the boy's left and girl's right shoulders and hips are apart. So, when you are travelling along the LOD, your bodies are pointing on the diagonals, i.e. boy facing DW and girl facing DC. The girls love this link step as they get to do a sharp head turn to the right, the move you see in all the movies! Get those necks warmed up girls – we don't want you in traction.

The link into closed promenade comes in two sections; the first being the link which consists of two moves and the second being the walks in closed promenade section, which consists of four moves. That's six moves in total, although they can be danced separately.

Link section for the first two moves
Move 1 *count Q*

■ *Boy LF forward*
Walk forwards with the left foot across the LOD.

■ *Girl RF back*
Walk backwards with the right foot across the LOD.

Move 2 *count Q*

■ *Boy RF side*
Step sideways with the right foot, turning your partner into the PP.

■ *Girl LF back*
Step sideways with your left foot into PP. Here's the fun bit – turn your head sharply to the right. So tango!

Walks in closed promenade section
Move 1 *count S*

■ *Boy LF forward*

Move your left foot forwards in PP along the LOD with your left foot pointing DW.

■ *Girl RF forward*

Move your right foot forwards in PP along the LOD with your right foot pointing DC.

Move 2 *count Q*

■ *Boy RF forward and across LF*

Bring your right foot towards your left foot and place it forwards across the left foot in PP.

■ *Girl LF forward and across RF*

Bring your left foot towards your right foot and place it forwards across the right foot in PP as you start to turn your body to the left.

Move 3 *count Q*

■ *Boy LF side*

Step to the side and slightly forwards with your left foot, leading your partner to turn to the left.

■ *Girl RF side*

As you continue your turn, step to the side and slightly back with the right foot with your body backing DW.

Move 4 *count S*

■ *Boy RF closes to LF*

Turn your body to the left and close your right foot to the left foot (slightly back) with your weight now on the right foot. Your body should be facing DW.

■ *Girl LF closes to RF*

As your body continues the turn, your left foot will close to the right foot (slightly forwards) with your weight now on the left foot. Your body should be backing DW.

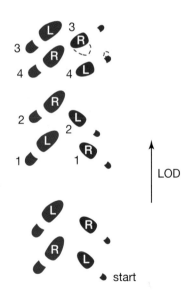

figure 13 walks in closed promenade

Amalgamations for the tango

Routine one

Rock turn

Link

Closed promenade

Routine two

Rock turn overturned on the last three steps so the boy ends facing DC

Basic reverse turn

Routine three

Two walks forward for the boy, backward for the girl

Link step overturned to end facing DC

Walks in closed promenade

Open reverse turn and closed finish

Each of the above tango routines can be repeated again and again around the room.

Note: You may be asking yourself what is overturn and how do I achieve it? Basically, overturn means that instead of turning a little, you turn a lot! It's just so you can end up facing the right direction for the next step you may wish to take, for instance, the rock turn finishes with the boy facing DW and the girl backing DW and you decide you would like to go into the basic reverse turn but 'oh dear' you notice that the basic reverse turn should start with the boy facing DC and the girl backing DC. What a dilemma! Overturn is your answer, all you do is during moves 6, 7 and 8 of the rock turn, just simply turn a bit more during each step until you end up facing or backing the direction you need to be in for the next step.

make up your own

Make up your own!

....

....

....

....

....

....

....

....

latin american

rumba
samba
cha cha cha
jive

rumba

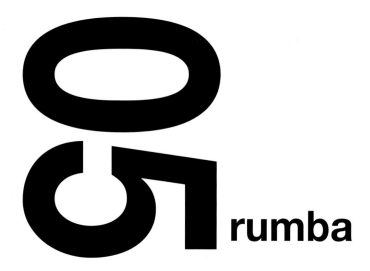

rumba

A little bit of raunchy history

This is most certainly the dance of love, and one of my personal favourites! It is the only slow dance in Latin American dancing, and some think it is the raunchiest. The rumba is a dance that has its origin with the African slaves imported into Cuba, whose dances emphasized the movements of the body rather than the feet. The tune was considered less important than the complex rhythms which were provided by a percussion of pots, spoons, bottles, etc. The rural form of the rumba in Cuba was described as a pantomime of barnyard animals, and was an exhibition rather than a participation dance. It was once said to be the simple portrayal of the pursuit of the hen bird by the cockerel because of the way the male dancer is constantly in pursuit of the female. It is definitely a fun dance for the girls who repeatedly lure the boy and then reject his advances in an act of intimate courtship.

The rumba arrived in the United States in the late 1920s and was first standardized by the British in 1946, based on what was known as a 'rumba box' which was couples dancing in a square pattern on the dance floor (an American pattern) as opposed to progressing around the entire dance floor.

What music do I dance to?

It's really important that you choose music you really love for the rumba. The rhythm and lyrics are also important because they should inspire you to move seductively and fluidly with your partner. The music for the rumba should be slow and sexy, about 26–7 bars per minute. It has a time signature of 4/4, which means that each bar of music has four equal beats: 1 2 3 4 – the first beat having an accent.

For the rumba, timing is important. Timing means the time it takes the dancer to complete the move on a certain count. In the rumba, the forward and backward steps are danced on beat 2. The side steps are danced over two beats, 4, 1. This is what gives the rumba its distinct feel and personality.

> **Track list**
>
> **15**   My introduction – getting you started.
>
> **16**   *Get Here*
>
> **17**   *Goldfinger*

Play track **15** of the CD to get you in the mood.

Hot rumba action

For the rumba I shall be using the term 'action' frequently. What I mean is the type of movement you use when you go into a step. You will want that hot hip action and, for the beginner, this can take a little time to master. Once you've got it, however, there will be no stopping you! You may even find yourself unknowingly practising this 'hot action' all over the house. Beware! It's addictive.

A good hip action is the result of good foot, ankle, knee and leg action, not the actual shaking or wiggling of the hips. The hip movement should occur naturally because of how your legs are moving. If you find you are forcing your hips into submission, you'll look and feel awkward. Give it time and it will come.

Forward and backward walks

This sounds simple, and it is! Each step is taken on the ball of the foot with a flexed knee. When the weight is taken onto the foot, the heel lowers and the knee straightens. The heel of the other foot is now released from the floor and the knee is flexed. At this point the hips move gently to the side of the straightened leg.

Forward walk

Easy, just step forwards and transfer your weight through your ball and heel. Make sure you release your other heel at the same time.

> **Top tip!**
>
> Use your ankles to control the transfer of body weight. This move should be smooth and fluid; don't let it be clunky by slamming your weight down on the foot carelessly.

Backward walk

Do the same as for the forward walk, but backward. This time, however, it's your front leg that ends with the heel slightly off the floor. It's this type of action that creates good hip action.

Basic rumba

The rumba is not a progressive dance; it doesn't move around the room. It's a dance where the couples occupy one part of the dance floor and are economical with their footwork and space.

Like the cha cha cha and jive, the rumba has no alignments which means as a non-progressive dance, the figures can be started and finished in any direction. That's one thing less for you to worry about and one more reason you'll find the basic rumba is to die for. The rumba turns gradually a quarter turn anticlockwise over six steps. You can repeat the basic rumba continuously. Full of passionate and persuasive hip action, and don't forget that the rumba is the dance of love!

The hold

Cuban dances have many different holds, the range of which are shown in 'The holds explained' on pages 15–19. It depends on what dance you are doing, but mostly you will always start with a normal hold or a close contact hold, what I call the 'breath-mint position'.

Close contact hold

The girl and boy are standing close together, about a hand's length between them – the breath-mint position! It is also a good idea to wear steel-cap toed shoes when learning this at home for the first time because the juxtaposition of the feet at such close proximity leaves the toes wide open for your partner to step on! The boy places his right hand high on the girl's shoulder blade. The girl lightly places her left hand on the boy's upper right arm. The boy raises his left hand to just below shoulder level with his elbow away from his body. The girl then places the fingers of her right hand between the thumb and index finger of the boy's left hand. The boy closes the fingers of his left hand to take hold. The girl is positioned slightly towards the boy's right.

> **Len's top tip**
>
> Remember while dancing the rumba
> To act like a cool cucumber
> With the correct hip action
> There will be lots of attraction
> And requests for your telephone number!

Latin love bunnies, prepare to dance and rule!

The Steps

Forward basic

This basic move is the best way of getting your body into that hot rumba rhythm. You are really going to love the feeling you get from it, and hopefully it will drive you wild with desire to do more!

Please refer to track **15** on the CD where I will talk you through the forward and back basics.

Nuno and Kerri will be demonstrating the Latin dances – keep an eye on how they hold themselves.

> **Note:** When you first try this next section, don't do the suggested turn. Just do the move plain and facing each other. Then, when you get the action of it and get used to the rhythm, put the turn in. You will find it a little disorientating at first, but with practice it will come. Be precise and deliberate! Start in a normal or beginner hold.

Count 1
Not danced.

Move 1 *count 2*
■ *Boy LF forward*
With your weight on the right foot, move forwards onto the left foot, allowing the toes to turn out slightly. Leave the right foot in place.

■ *Girl RF back*
With your weight on the left foot move back onto the right foot, leaving the left foot in place.

move 1

Move 2 *count 3*

■ *Boy RF back*

Transfer weight back onto the right foot, leaving the left foot in place.

■ *Girl LF forward*

Transfer weight forwards onto the left foot, allowing the toes to turn out slightly and leaving the right foot in place.

move 2

move 3

Move 3 *count 4, 1*

■ *Boy LF side*

Place the inside edge of the ball of the left foot to the side as you turn a little to the left foot.

■ *Girl RF side*

Place the inside edge of the ball of the right foot to the side as you turn a little to the left and roll your weight on to the right foot.

How was that? I hope you were looking deep into the eyes of your partner trying to create some sort of chemistry. If you were only worried about the steps, go back and this time try it with some emotion. It's about seduction, as is the back basic. If you feel you have got it, then go on to learn the back basic.

Back basic

Count 1

Not danced.

Move 1 *count 2*

■ *Boy RF back*

Move back onto the right foot, leaving the left foot in place.

■ *Girl LF forward*

Move forwards onto the left foot, allowing the toes to turn out slightly and leaving the right foot in place.

move 1

move 2

Move 2 *count 3*

■ *Boy LF forward*

Transfer your weight forwards onto the left foot, allowing the toes to turn out slightly and leaving the right foot in place.

■ *Girl RF back*

Transfer your weight back onto the right foot, leaving the left foot in place.

Move 3 *count 4, 1*

■ *Boy RF side*
Place the inside edge of the ball of the right foot to the side as you turn a little to the left and roll your weight on to the right foot.

■ *Girl LF side*
Place the inside edge of the ball of the left foot to the side as you turn a little to the left and roll your weight on to the left foot.

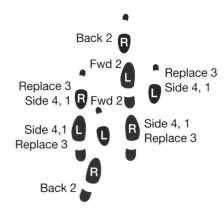

Back 2 **R**

Fwd 2

Replace 3
Side 4, 1

Replace 3
Side 4, 1 **R** Fwd 2 **L**

Side 4,1 **L** **L** **R** Side 4, 1
Replace 3   Replace 3

R

Back 2

figure 14   forward and back basic (with the counts)

Note: This diagram shows you the foot positions with the counts not the move numbers, just so you can get an idea of how the rumba starts on count 2 and the side steps are taken over two counts of the music, 4, 1. After trying this a few times, and if you feel confident with the music, try putting in a gradual turn to the left.

move 3

Side step

In order to make your side step sizzle, keep your steps small and remember when you transfer your weight from one foot to another that it's a slow and seductive two beats. There is nothing more unattractive than big old clumpy steps.

Side step

Place the foot in position to the side, then transfer the body weight onto that foot but this time, over two beats of the music. It's slower than the forward and backward walks.

Count 1

Not danced.

Move 1 *count 2*

■ *Boy LF side*

Start with your weight on the right foot, then place your left foot to the side.

■ *Girl RF side*

Start with your weight on the left foot, then place your right foot to the side.

Move 2 *count 3*

■ *Boy RF closes to LF*

Close your right foot to your left foot.

■ *Girl LF closes to RF*

Close your left foot to your right foot.

Move 3 *count 4, 1, 2*

■ ■ *Both*

Repeat moves 1 and 2 twice.

Cucaracha

This move is deliciously simple and named after the cockroach – the Spanish word, *cucaracha* means cockroach. It's a useful 'holding pattern' dance until you decide what step may follow, and it's easy but very effective.

Side cucaracha to the left

Count 1

Not danced.

Move 1 *count 2*

■ *Boy LF side*

Start with your weight on the right foot, then step sideways with your left foot placing a little weight onto it.

■ *Girl RF side*

Start with your weight on the left foot, then step sideways with your right foot, placing a little weight onto it.

Move 2 *count 3*

■ *Boy weight to RF*

Transfer your weight onto the right foot.

■ *Girl weight to LF*

Transfer your weight onto the left foot.

Move 3 *counts 4, 1*

■ *Boy LF closes to RF*

Close the left foot to your right foot.

■ *Girl RF closes to LF*

Close the right foot to your left foot.

Note: As soon as you've finished, go directly to the side cucaracha to the right.

Side cucaracha to the right

Start as side cucaracha to the left, but your weight will be on the opposite foot as this is a continuation of the figure.

Count 1

Not danced.

Move 1 *count 2*

■ *Boy RF side*

Start with your weight on the left foot then step sideways with the right foot, placing a little weight onto it.

■ *Girl LF side*

Start with your weight on the right foot, then step sideways with the left foot, placing a little weight onto it.

Move 2 *count 3*

■ *Boy weight to LF*

Transfer your weight onto the left foot.

■ *Girl weight to RF*

Transfer your weight onto the right foot.

Move 3 *counts 4, 1*

■ *Boy RF closes to LF*

Close the right foot to your left foot.

■ *Girl LF closes to RF*

Close the left foot to your right foot.

> **Note:** You can follow this figure with a forward basic for the boy (back basic for the girl), so go for it!

The New York

Frank Sinatra can't take the credit for this one, and neither can Liza Minnelli, although I suspect both have danced it, and they sure sang about it! Our New York developed on the back streets of New York City in the Hispanic neighbourhoods – very *West Side Story*. If you've never seen the film, rent it today; it's an important classic and full of Latin dance and rhythms to give you great inspiration. I was lucky enough to be the associate director and choreographer on the stage musical in the West End in London and found that it has some of the most explosive, extraordinary and honest choreography that has ever graced a musical stage. When you watch the musical you feel as though you are there in the streets, and you get the atmosphere and earthy qualities of true Latin spirit and struggle. It is also a Romeo and Juliet love story which is exactly what we want to achieve in the rumba, the dance of love!

The New York is one of the most classic steps, and to dance it start in a normal or double hand hold with feet slightly apart.

Count 1

Not danced.

Move 1 *count 2*

■ *Boy LF forward turn R*

Facing your partner with your weight on the right foot, release hold of the right hand and make a quarter of a turn to the right while moving forwards with your left foot to end in the left S×S position.

■ *Girl RF forward turn L*

Facing your partner with your weight on the left foot, release hold of the left hand and make a quarter of a turn to the left while moving forwards with your right foot to end in the left S×S position.

move 1

move 2

Move 2 *count 3*

■ *Boy weight to RF*

Transfer your weight onto the right foot.

■ *Girl weight to LF*

Transfer your weight onto the left foot.

Move 3 *counts 4, 1*

■ *Boy LF side turn L*

Step sideways with the left foot and turn a quarter turn to the left, at the same time regaining the double hand hold with your partner.

■ *Girl RF side turn R*

Step sideways with the right foot making a quarter turn to the right, at the same time regaining the double hand hold with your partner.

move 3

move 4

Move 4 *count 2*

■ *Boy RF forward*

Release hold of the left hand and make a quarter of a turn to the left while moving forwards with your right foot to end in the right S×S position.

■ *Girl LF forward*

Release hold of the right hand and make a quarter of a turn to the right while moving forwards with your left foot to end in the right S×S position.

Move 5 *count 3*

■ *Boy weight to LF*
Transfer weight back to the left foot.

■ *Girl weight to RF*
Transfer weight back to the right foot.

move 5

move 6

Move 6 *count 4, 1*

■ *Boy RF side turn R*
Step sideways with the right foot and turn a quarter turn to the right, at the same time regaining the double hand hold with your partner.

■ *Girl LF side turn L*
Step sideways with the left foot making a quarter turn to the left, at the same time regaining the double hand hold.

The fan

This step is a great way of getting into other dance positions. Like a fan, it opens up on move 3 – the fan position. It consists of three moves and the rhythm goes like this: 2, 3, 4, 1.

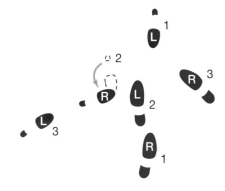

figure 15 the fan

move 1

Count 1

Not danced.

Move 1 *count 2*

■ *Boy RF back*

Step back onto the right foot, leaving the left foot in place. At the same time, you need to lead your partner forwards towards you.

■ *Girl LF forward*

Step forwards onto the left foot in between your partner's feet.

Move 2 *count 3*

■ *Boy LF forward*

Transfer your weight forwards onto the left foot as you release the hold with the right hand.

■ *Girl RF back*

Step backwards with the right foot at right angles to your partner and start to turn to the left.

> **Note:** Nuno's and Kerri's hand and arm position on move 2.

move 2

move 3

Move 3 *count 4, 1*

■ *Boy RF side*

Place the inside edge of the ball of your right foot to the side and roll your weight onto the right foot, looking deep into the eyes of your partner! Extend your left arm as your partner moves away.

■ *Girl LF back*

Move back onto the left foot, still at right angles to your partner, leaving the right foot in place. Release and extend the left hand out to the side as you do so.

Congratulations! That's the fan position. You can now do a forward and back basic into a fan. Let's go on and try something a little more challenging for the girls.

The hockey stick

I know this is a weird name for a dance move and no, you are not going to grab a hockey stick and hit your partner over the head with it. Instead, you'll create a pattern on the floor that resembles the *shape* of a hockey stick when you complete the move. This move is set over a series of six moves and eight counts (that's 2×4 counts) and, as normal in the rumba, we start the move on count 2 and it follows the fan.

The rhythm goes like this: 2, 3, 4, 1, 2, 3, 4, 1.

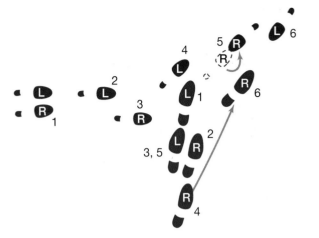

figure 16   the hockey stick

Count 1

Not danced.

Move 1 *count 2*

■ *Boy LF forward*

From the fan position, step forwards onto the left foot, leaving the right foot in place.

■ *Girl RF closes to LF*

From the fan position, close your right foot to your left foot.

Move 2 *count 3*

■ *Boy weight to RF*

Transfer weight back onto your right foot, leaving the left foot in place. Bring your partner towards you.

■ *Girl LF forward*

Walk forwards onto the left foot.

Move 3 *count 4, 1*

■ Boy LF closes to RF

Close your left foot to your right foot and transfer your weight onto the left foot. At this point you need to make a hand adjustment so you don't break each other's wrists.

■ Girl RF forward

Walk forwards onto the right foot.

> **Note:** The boy starts the move with the palm of his left hand facing skywards as he brings the girl into him on move 2. On move 3 he raises his left arm and, at the same time, rotates his hand towards himself to accommodate the girl (as you would if shielding your eyes from the sun), and then away from himself to resolve in a normal palm to palm hold with the thumb down.

Move 4 *count 2*

■ Boy RF back

Take a small step back onto the right foot as you turn a bit to the right, leading your partner past you, raising your hand above her head as she does so.

■ Girl LF forward turn L

Walk forwards onto the left foot and start to turn to the left in front of your partner.

Move 5 *count 3*

■ Boy weight to LF

Transfer your weight forwards onto your left foot, leading your partner forwards away from you.

■ Girl RF forward turn L

As you continue the turn to the left step forwards onto your right foot, turning in towards your partner.

> **Note:** This forward step for the girl is the part of the hockey stick shape that curves at the end of the stick, hence the name!

Move 6 *count 4, 1*

■ Boy RF forward

Step forwards on your right foot to end in an open facing position. On completion of your partner's step lower your left hand to waist height.

■ Girl LF back

Step backwards on your left foot to end facing your partner.

> **Note:** The hockey stick in the rumba and cha cha cha can only ever be danced from a fan position.

The Alemana turn

This is a fierce turn for the girls and you're not going to want to stop doing it. Be warned, however, too much of a good thing can be dangerous! The simplicity in this turn makes it a great one to start with and for the girls all it is are three walks forward turning under the boy's arm.

There are six steps to this figure and the rhythm goes: 2, 3, 4, 1, 2, 3, 4, 1.

Count 1

Not danced.

Move 1 *count 2*

■ *Boy LF forward*

With your weight on the right foot step forwards with the left foot.

■ *Girl RF back*

With your weight on the left foot step backwards with the right foot.

move 1

move 2

Move 2 *count 3*

■ *Boy weight to RF*

Transfer your weight onto the right foot.

■ *Girl LF forward*

Transfer your weight forwards onto the left foot.

Move 3 *counts 4, 1*

■ *Boy LF closes to RF*

Close your left foot to the right foot and raise your left arm (in preparation for your partner to turn under), releasing hold with the right hand.

■ *Girl RF side turn R*

Take a small step to the side with the right foot and start turning to the right, releasing hold with the left hand.

move 3

move 4

Move 4 *count 2*

■ *Boy RF back*

Step backwards with the right foot and lead your partner to turn right underneath your left arm.

■ *Girl LF forward*

Step forwards with the left foot, continuing to turn.

Move 5 *count 3*

■ *Boy weight to LF*

Transfer your weight forwards onto the left foot, circling the left hand clockwise.

■ *Girl RF forward turn R*

Step forwards onto the right foot and continue the turn to the right.

move 5

move 6

Move 6 *counts 4, 1*

■ *Boy RF closes to LF*

Close your right foot to the left foot as you lower your left arm, bringing your partner to the normal hold.

■ *Girl LF side*

Completing the turn to the right, step sideways with the left foot ending up facing your partner and taking up the normal hold again.

Opening out – right and left

Guys, you've now got it easy and it's time for the girls to do all the work! The boys will do the side cucaracha left and right while the girls will do the fancy stuff. This figure consists of six steps and the rhythm goes: 2, 3, 4, 1, 2, 3, 4, 1. Take a look at this:

Count 1

Not danced.

Move 1 *count 2*

■ *Boy LF side*

Start with your weight on the right foot, then step sideways with the left foot, placing a little weight onto it, extending your left arm outwards.

■ *Girl RF back*

Start with your weight on the left foot then step backwards with the right foot, turning to the right, to end at right angles to your partner, extending your right arm outwards.

Move 2 *count 3*

■ *Boy weight to RF*

Transfer your weight onto the right foot.

■ *Girl weight to LF*

Transfer your weight onto the left foot.

Move 3 *counts 4, 1*

■ *Boy LF closes to RF*

Close your left foot to the right foot, placing your free hand on your partner's shoulder blades to help guide her.

■ *Girl RF side*

Turning to the left, step sideways with your right foot, end facing your partner, placing your free arm onto his left upper arm.

Move 4 *count 2*

■ *Boy RF side*

Step sideways with your right foot, placing a little weight onto it and extend your right arm outwards.

■ *Girl LF back*

Step back with your left foot as you turn to the left, to end at right angles to your partner and extend your left arm outwards.

Move 5 *count 3*

■ *Boy weight to LF*

Transfer your weight onto the left foot.

■ *Girl weight to RF*

Transfer your weight onto the right foot.

Move 6 *counts 4, 1*

■ *Boy RF closes to LF*

Close your right foot to the left foot.

■ *Girl LF side*

Turning to the right, step sideways with the left foot to end facing your partner in the normal hold.

Note: You can now follow this with a forward basic and then a back basic.

Hand to hand

Start this move in a double hand hold. It has six steps and the rhythm goes: 2, 3, 4, 1, 2, 3, 4, 1.

Count 1

Not danced.

Move 1 *count 2*

■ *Boy LF back R S×S*

Facing your partner, with your weight on the right foot, release hold of the left hand and make a quarter of a turn to the left while stepping backwards with the left foot to end in right S×S position.

■ *Girl RF back*

Facing your partner, with your weight on the left foot, release hold of the right hand and make a quarter of a turn to the right while stepping backwards with the right foot to end in right S×S position.

Move 2 *count 3*

■ *Boy weight to RF*

Transfer your weight onto the right foot.

■ *Girl weight to LF*

Transfer your weight onto the left foot.

Move 3 *counts 4, 1*

■ *Boy LF side*

Step sideways with the left foot as you turn a quarter turn to the right to face your partner and regaining the double hand hold.

■ *Girl RF side*

Step sideways with your right foot as you turn a quarter turn to the left to face your partner and regaining the double hand hold.

Move 4 *count 2*

■ *Boy RF back L S×S*

Release hold of the right hand and make a quarter of a turn to the right while stepping backwards with the right foot to end in left S×S position.

■ *Girl LF back*

Release hold of the left hand and make a quarter of a turn to the left while stepping backwards with the left foot to end in left S×S position.

Move 5 *count 3*

■ *Boy weight to LF*

Transfer your weight onto the left foot.

■ *Girl weight to RF*

Transfer your weight onto the right foot.

Move 6 *counts 4, 1*

■ *Boy RF side*

Step sideways with the right foot as you turn a quarter turn to the left to face your partner and regaining the double hand hold.

■ *Girl LF side*

Step sideways with your left foot as you turn a quarter turn to the right to face your partner and regaining the double hand hold.

amalgamations

Amalgamations for the rumba
Routine one

Forward basic

Back basic

New York × 4

Routine two

Cucaracha left

Alemana turn

Hand to hand × 4

Routine three

Forward basic

Fan

Hockey stick

Alemana turn

Opening out right and left

Make up your own!

....

....

....

....

....

....

....

....

samba

samba

A little bit of sizzling history

The samba is a carnival dance from Brazil, but it didn't start life that way. It was originally performed by African slaves who worked on the sugar plantations in a place called Bahia, in the north of Brazil. The slaves brought drums with them called 'Batuque', creating amazing percussive rhythms that they would dance to as a means of escapism, but the rhythms were also used for ritualistic purposes when aromatic herbs were held in each hand and waved under the nose of the dancer to induce an intoxicated, drug-like state. The word for dance in the native language of the slaves was *semba* so you can see how the samba became the national dance of Brazil.

The samba used to be a solo dance but became the Latin dance that we recognize today with the help of the Maxixe (pronounced mah-chee-chay) dance. The Maxixe came from Brazil where it was a wild folk dance combining syncopation with the rhythm of the Cuban Habañera and the movements of the European polka. It became popular in Brazilian ballrooms, and then the USA took to it just before the First World War. The samba was introduced in 1939 at the New York World Fair, and it was this version that ended up making its way to Europe before the Second World War. Does anyone remember a crazy woman from the old films who wore fruit on her head and danced like a lunatic? Her name was Carmen Miranda; she must take some blame for the success and major rise in the popularity of the samba, as must Fred Astaire and Ginger Rogers with

the movie *Flying Down to Rio*, which has some really cool moves. The samba features in the incredible carnival in Rio, which takes place every February, turning the vibrant city of Rio de Janeiro into a raucous knees-up. What makes the samba so attractive and gives it an international appeal is the energy and fun-loving street dancing and fantastic outfits. The samba you are about to learn is not the improvised carnival party dance, but a simplified ballroom basic that retains the heart and soul of the dance. It's party time, people!

What music do I dance to?

The time signature for the samba is 2/4, which means it has two beats to every bar of music. There are three different rhythms for you to familiarize yourself with. The first one we should tackle is the 'one a two'. It is like the tango but there is a special new beat you have to learn, and that's the quarter beat. We pronounce the quarter beat as 'a'. In order to count the rhythm of the samba you say 'one a two'. The values for the beats go like this:

- Count 1 = $^3/_4$ of the beat
- Count a = $^1/_4$ of the beat
- Count 2 = 1 whole beat.

This makes a total of two beats.

As you can see, the rhythm of the first beat is split unevenly with the count 'a' stealing its quarter beat from count 1. That's what makes the rhythm so fabulous and intoxicating. In order to confuse you even more, the samba rhythm changes depending on what moves you are doing. Don't panic if you're not musically minded, when you hear the rhythms it will all become clear.

Samba's other rhythm is an easy one, it goes like this 'one, two':

- Count 1 = 1 whole beat
- Count 2 = 1 whole beat.

This makes a total of two beats.

Here is a list of what moves go with what rhythms:

Counts 'one, two'
- Side basic
- Natural basic
- Reverse basic.

One beat is given to each step in these figures.

Counts 'one a two'
- Alternative side basic
- Alternative natural basic
- Alternative reverse basic.

Just one more samba rhythm to learn and you're done! This rhythm is used in the Corta Jaca which is like the tango, so you should be a little familiar with it. In this dance we use whole and half beats. It's said like this: 'one, two and one and two and'. Broken down, the beats measure out like this:

- Count 1   = 1 whole beat
- Count 2   = $\frac{1}{2}$ beat
- Count and = $\frac{1}{2}$ beat
- Count 1   = $\frac{1}{2}$ beat
- Count and = $\frac{1}{2}$ beat
- Count two = $\frac{1}{2}$ beat
- Count and = $\frac{1}{2}$ beat.

This makes a total of four beats in two bars.

The tempo of the samba can be anything between 48–56 bars per minute. That's pretty fast!

Track list

18   My introduction – getting you started.

19   *Independent Women*

20   *Axel F*

Listen and get all funked up to track **18**. Try counting some of the rhythms you've just learnt to the music.

The hold

The hold for the samba is the same as for the rumba (see page 99).

Bounce!

Hot and horny knee action is required for the samba. It's known as 'samba bounce action', and it's extremely important because it gives the samba its unique look and feel. The action comes from the flexing and straightening of the knees or what, in ballet terms, is known as 'plié' – basically the bending of the knees! You don't want to exaggerate this action, but you do want it to be a gentle, rhythmic action that is felt through the knees and ankles, with a slight elevation at the end of each beat of music. Regarding your footwork, the samba is danced ball to flat foot except when you do your quarter beats, which you dance on the balls of your feet.

Basic bounce

The basic bounce goes with the counts 'one, two' that we learnt in the 'What music do I dance to?' section. There are two steps to every bar of music, and what happens to the legs between these steps is what we're now interested in:

- On the step, bend your knees
- Between the step, straighten your knees.

Alternative basic bounce

This is like the basic bounce but has an alternative rhythm, and it goes with counts 'one a two'. There are three steps to each bar of music, and this is what happens to the legs on those steps:

- Count 1: on the first step, bend your knees
- Count a: on the second step, straighten your knees
- Count 2: on the third step, bend your knees
- Between the third step and the following step, straighten your knees.

There are many basic steps to learn in the samba, but don't let what seems like an enormous amount of information put you off – you'll find the steps really simple and enjoyable to do. Once you've got the steps under your belt and in your body, you won't want to stop dancing. The samba really is a dance you can literally just leap onto the floor with. Embrace it, as it's about to belong to you!

Len's top tip

The samba which comes from Brazil
Danced well will give you a thrill
You need speed and control
And to dance from your soul
But too much bounce will soon make you ill.

The steps

Natural basic

Let's begin with the easy stuff and work ourselves into a hot, steamy lather later on. There are four steps in the natural basic, the rhythm is even and goes like this: 1, 2, 1, 2.

Familiarize yourself with the rhythms on track **18** on the CD and then have a go at the natural basic.

Begin in the normal hold and use a little basic bounce.

Move 1 *count 1*

■ *Boy RF forward*

With your body facing the LOD and your weight on the left foot, step forwards onto the right foot.

■ *Girl LF back*

With your body backing the LOD and your weight on the right foot, step backwards with the left foot.

Move 2 *count 2*

■ *Boy LF closes to RF*

Close your left foot to the right foot, applying a little pressure but without any weight.

■ *Girl RF closes to LF*

Close your right foot to the left foot, applying a little pressure but without any weight.

Move 3 *count 1*

■ *Boy LF back*

Step backwards with the left foot.

■ *Girl RF forward*

Step forwards with the right foot.

Move 4 *count 2*

■ *Boy RF closes to LF*

Close your right foot to the left foot, applying a little pressure but without weight.

■ *Girl LF closes to RF*

Close your left foot to the right foot, applying a little pressure but without weight.

Try this a few times while you get your bounce action sorted out, then when you feel confident, turn the whole figure gradually to the right. This basic can be turned or not, depending on how you feel on the day.

Congratulations! You're now on a journey to samba satisfaction. Now, let's try it with a different rhythm.

Alternative natural basic

There are six steps in this figure and the rhythm goes like this: 1 a 2, 1 a 2.

As with the natural basic, start in a normal hold but this time use alternative basic bounce. You can turn this figure gradually to the right if the mood takes you.

Move 1 *count 1*

■ *Boy RF forward*

Start facing the LOD with your weight on the left foot, then step forwards with the right foot.

■ *Girl LF back*

Start backing the LOD with your weight on the right foot, then step backwards with the left foot.

Move 2 *count a*

■ *Boy LF closes to RF*

Close your left foot to the right foot and transfer your weight onto the left foot.

■ *Girl RF closes to LF*

Close your right foot to the left foot and transfer your weight onto the right foot.

Move 3 *count 2*

■ *Boy weight to RF*

Transfer your weight back onto the right foot.

■ *Girl weight to LF*

Transfer your weight back onto the left foot.

Move 4 *count 1*

■ *Boy LF back*

Step backwards with the left foot.

■ *Girl RF forward*

Step forwards with the right foot.

Move 5 *count a*

■ *Boy RF closes to LF*

Close your right foot to the left foot and transfer your weight onto the right foot.

■ *Girl LF closes to RF*

Close your left foot to the right foot and transfer your weight onto the left foot.

Move 6 *count 2*

■ *Boy weight to LF*

Transfer your weight back onto the left foot.

■ *Girl weight to RF*

Transfer your weight back onto the right foot.

Reverse basic

You'll be thrilled to know that the reverse basic is the same as the natural basic but danced with the other foot!

This step has a basic bounce action and has four steps with the rhythm: 1, 2, 1, 2.

If you're up to it, why not throw in a gradual turn to the left this time? Like the other steps you can choose to do it with or without the turn.

Move 1 *count 1*

■ *Boy LF forward*

With your body facing the LOD and your weight on the right foot, step forwards onto the left foot.

■ *Girl RF back*

With your body backing the LOD and your weight on the left foot, step backwards with the right foot.

Move 2 *count 2*

■ *Boy RF closes to LF*

Close your right foot to your left foot, applying a little pressure but without weight.

■ *Girl LF closes to RF*

Close your left foot to your right foot, applying a little pressure but without weight.

Move 3 *count 1*

■ *Boy RF back*

Step backwards with your right foot.

■ *Girl LF forward*

Step forwards with your left foot.

Move 4 *count 2*

■ *Boy LF closes to RF*

Close your left foot to your right foot, applying a little pressure but without any weight.

■ *Girl RF closes to LF*

Close your right foot to your left foot, applying a little pressure but without any weight.

Alternative reverse basic

The alternative reverse basic is the same as the alternative natural basic but danced with the other foot!

This basic is all about alternative basic bounce (ABB) and, like all other alternatives, it has six steps and the rhythm goes like this: 1 a 2, 1 a 2.

Move 1 *count 1*

■ *Boy LF forward*

Start facing the LOD with your weight on the right foot, then step forwards with the left foot.

■ *Girl RF back*

Start backing the LOD with your weight on the left foot, then step backwards with the right foot.

Move 2 *count a*

■ *Boy RF closes to LF*

Close your right foot to the left foot and transfer your weight onto the right foot.

■ *Girl LF closes to RF*

Close your left foot to the right foot and transfer your weight onto the left foot.

Move 3 *count 2*

■ *Boy weight to LF*

Transfer your weight back onto the left foot.

■ *Girl weight to RF*

Transfer your weight back onto the right foot.

Move 4 *count 1*

■ *Boy RF back*

Step backwards with the right foot.

■ *Girl LF forward*

Step forwards with the left foot.

Move 5 *count a*

■ *Boy LF closes to RF*

Close your left foot to the right foot and transfer your weight onto the left foot.

■ *Girl RF closes to LF*

Close your right foot to the left foot and transfer your weight onto the right foot.

Move 6 *count 2*

■ *Boy weight to RF*

Transfer your weight onto the right foot.

■ *Girl weight to LF*

Transfer your weight onto the left foot.

Side basic with basic bounce

We can now take the dance sideways. Both boy and girl begin in a normal hold for this step. It consists of four steps and the rhythm goes like this: 1, 2, 1, 2.

Move 1 *count 1*

■ *Boy LF side*

Start by FW with your weight on the right foot, then step sideways with the left foot.

■ *Girl RF side*

Start by BW with your weight on the left foot, then step sideways with the right foot.

Move 2 *count 2*

■ *Boy RF closes to LF*

Close your right foot to the left foot, applying a little pressure but without weight.

■ *Girl LF closes to RF*

Close your left foot to the right foot, applying a little pressure but without weight.

Move 3 *count 1*

■ *Boy RF side*

Step sideways with the right foot.

■ *Girl LF side*

Step sideways with the left foot.

Move 4 *count 2*

■ *Boy LF closes to RF*

Close your left foot to the right foot, applying a little pressure but without any weight.

■ *Girl RF closes to LF*

Close your right foot to the left foot, applying a little pressure but without any weight.

Side basic with alternative basic bounce

Start this in a normal hold and go for that audacious alternative rhythm: 1 a 2, 1 a 2.

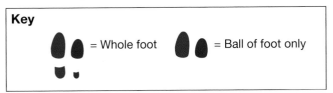

Key	
= Whole foot	= Ball of foot only

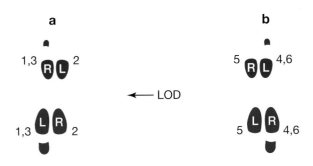

figure 17 side basic with alternative basic bounce
a left **b** right

Move 1 *count 1*

■ *Boy LF side*
Start by FW with your weight on the right foot, then step sideways with the left foot.

■ *Girl RF side*
Start by BW with your weight on your left foot, then step sideways with the right foot.

Move 2 *count a*

■ *Boy RF closes to LF*
Close your right foot to the left foot and transfer your weight onto the right foot.

■ *Girl LF closes to RF*
Close your left foot to the right foot and transfer your weight onto the left foot.

Move 3 *count 2*

■ *Boy weight to LF*
Transfer your weight back onto the left foot.

■ *Girl weight to RF*
Transfer your weight back onto the right foot.

Move 4 *count 1*

■ *Boy RF side*
Step sideways with the right foot.

■ *Girl LF side*
Step sideways with the left foot.

Move 5 *count a*

■ *Boy LF closes to RF*

Close your left foot to the right foot and transfer your weight onto the left foot.

■ *Girl RF closes to LF*

Close your right foot to the left foot and transfer your weight onto the right foot.

Move 6 *count 2*

■ *Boy weight to RF*

Transfer your weight back onto the right foot.

■ *Girl weight to LF*

Transfer your weight back onto the left foot.

Progressive basic

In the progressive basic you need to reduce the amount of bounce. It consists of four steps and the rhythm goes like this: 1, 2, 1, 2.

Move 1 *count 1*

■ *Boy RF forward*

With your body facing DW and your weight on the left foot, step forwards onto the right foot.

■ *Girl LF back*

With your body backing DW and your weight on the right foot, step backwards with the left foot.

Move 2 *count 2*

■ *Boy LF closes to RF*

Close your left foot to the right foot, applying a little pressure but without any weight.

■ *Girl RF closes to LF*

Close your right foot to the left foot, applying a little pressure but without any weight.

Move 3 *count 1*

■ *Boy LF side*

Step sideways with the left foot.

■ *Girl RF side*

Step sideways with the right foot.

Move 4 *count 2*

■ *Boy RF closes to LF*

Close your right foot to the left foot, applying a little pressure but without weight.

■ *Girl LF closes to RF*

Close your left foot to the right foot, applying a little pressure but without weight.

> **Note:** I've suggested that this figure starts with your bodies facing DW or backing DW, but you could choose to start it facing or backing the LOD if you fancied.

Well done! You have successfully learnt all your basic steps. I know it was a hard slog, but you'll see that it was worth every headache and blister. Now we can start running some of the figures together. Why don't you try a natural basic into the progressive basic?

Whisk to right

This whisk is nothing like the whisk you learnt in the waltz so take time to study it to avoid any sort of confusion. The samba whisk has a three-step movement and it uses alternative basic bounce rhythmically doing: 1 a 2.

Start in a normal hold.

Move 1 *count 1*

■ *Boy RF side*

Start by FW with your weight on the left foot, then step sideways with the right foot.

■ *Girl LF side*

Start by BW with your weight on the right foot, then step sideways with the left foot.

move 1

move 2

> **Note:** Nuno and Kerri are demonstrating an alternative hand hold you may wish to try out.

Move 2 *count a*

■ *Boy LF behind RF*

Place your left foot (left toe to right heel) behind the right foot.

■ *Girl RF behind LF*

Place your right foot (right toe to left heel) behind the left foot.

Move 3 *count 2*

■ *Boy weight to RF*
Transfer your weight onto the right foot.

■ *Girl weight to LF*
Transfer your weight onto the left foot.

Follow with a whisk to the left (see right).

move 3

Whisk to left

This is the same as the whisk to the right, just danced on the opposite side!

Move 1 *count 1*

■ *Boy LF side*
Start by FW with your weight on the right foot, then step sideways with the left foot.

■ *Girl RF side*
Start by BW with your weight on the left foot, then step sideways with the right foot.

Move 2 *count a*

■ *Boy RF behind LF*
Place your right foot (right toe to left heel) behind the left foot.

■ *Girl LF behind RF*
Place your left foot (left toe to right heel) behind the right foot.

Move 3 *count 2*

■ *Boy weight to LF*
Transfer your weight onto the left foot.

■ *Girl weight to RF*
Transfer your weight onto the right foot.

> **Note:** For the whisk, when you move sideways, do so ball to flat foot. In move 2, when you cross your foot behind, place the toe of that foot just behind the heel of the other foot. Also allow the heel of the other foot to lift a little from the floor.

Try putting some of these figures together: natural basic into a whisk to the right or maybe do a whisk left and then a whisk right. Then follow with a reverse basic.

Samba walks in promenade position (PP)

The previous moves have all been on the spot and I think it's high time we started moving around the dance floor to get the blood going and kick up a bit of dust. Samba walks are perfect for that.

It's a six-step scenario that includes a left foot samba walk and a right foot samba walk with the rhythm: 1 a 2, 1 a 2.

The walk uses just a small amount of alternative basic bounce (ABB). Don't go overboard on the alternative basic bounce as you wouldn't want to do yourself or others a mischief.

In order to dance this figure both the girl and boy need to end up in PP, which you should be totally at home with by now. Maybe you've completed a side basic or a whisk to the right, in which case you need to modify the end of your preceding figure to finish in PP, facing the LOD.

Move 1 *count 1*
■ *Boy LF forward*
Start in PP facing LOD with your weight on the right foot, then step forwards onto the left foot. End with your hips over your foot.

■ *Girl RF forward*
Start in PP facing the LOD with your weight on the left foot, then step forwards onto the right foot. End with your hips over your foot.

Move 2 *count a*
■ *Boy RF back*
Extend your right foot back, putting part of your weight onto it.

■ *Girl LF back*
Extend your left foot back, putting part of your weight onto it.

Move 3 *count 2*
■ *Boy LF towards RF*
Pull your left foot slightly back towards the right foot.

■ *Girl RF towards LF*
Pull your right foot slightly back towards the left foot.

> **Note:** That completes the left foot samba walk. Continue with the next move to complete the right foot samba walk.

Move 4 *count 1*
■ *Boy RF forward*
Step forwards onto the right foot. End with your hips over your foot.

■ *Girl LF forward*
Step forwards onto the left foot. End with your hips over your foot.

Move 5 *count a*
■ *Boy LF back*
Extend your left foot back, putting part of your weight onto it.

■ *Girl RF back*
Extend your right foot back, putting part of your weight onto it.

Move 6 *count 2*
■ *Boy RF towards LF*
Pull your right foot slightly back towards the left foot.

■ *Girl LF towards RF*
Pull your left foot slightly back towards the right foot.

You can go ahead now and do this figure twice more, ending in PP. Then go into a side basic or left whisk, turning to face your partner.

Volta

So, what's a volta? It was a very fast dance popular in Italy during the sixteenth and seventeenth centuries; pieces of music written for the volta were also called 'voltas' and were in a triple time rhythm of the dance. 'Volta' also means a single playing of a passage of music that may then be repeated.

The word 'volta' translates as 'the turn' and, even in its earliest days, the dance appears to have involved the couple turning as they danced. In order to do this in the volta, the partners had to hold each other in such a close embrace that many declared it immoral. Louis XIII (1601–43) banned the waltzing volta from court on this account. The volta in the samba has nothing to do with the waltzing volta of Louis XIII's time, apart from the fact that it turns! It is now, without a doubt, a classic move in the samba and the rhythm is: 1 a 2 a 1 a 2.

This consists of seven steps during which you can make a gradual turn. Think of it as a gentle curve. All the voltas described use alternative basic bounce (ABB).

Volta travelling left

The volta travelling left has a gradual turn to the left, making up to three eighths of a turn, and the timing for this figure is: 1 a 2 a 1 a 2.

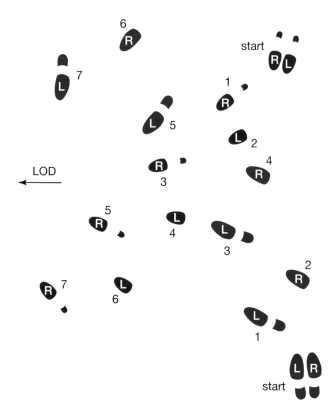

figure 18 volta turning left

Move 1 *count 1*

■ *Boy LF in front RF*

With your body FW and your weight on the right foot, starting a turn to the left, place your left foot in front of the right foot (left heel to right toe).

■ *Girl RF in front LF*

With your body BW and your weight on the left foot, starting a turn to the left, place your right foot in front of the left foot (right heel to left toe).

move 1

move 2

> **Note:** In the photograph above you can see that Nuno and Kerri have stepped across more than normal to clearly demonstrate the crossing action of the feet.

Move 2 *count a*

■ *Boy RF side*

Step sideways and a little back with the right foot, turning the toe out.

■ *Girl LF side*

Step sideways and a little back with the left foot, turning the toe out.

Move 3 *count 2*

- **■ *Boy drag LF front RF***

Drag your left foot in front of your right foot (left heel to right toe).

- **■ *Girl drag RF front LF***

Drag your right foot in front of your left foot (right heel to left toe).

> **Note:** The next four moves are simply repeats of moves 2 and 3 as follows.

move 3

Move 4 *count a*

- **■ *Boy RF side***

Step sideways and a little back with the right foot, turning the toe out.

- **■ *Girl LF side***

Step sideways and a little back with the left foot, turning the toe out.

Move 5 *count 1*

- **■ *Boy drag LF front RF***

Drag your left foot in front of the right foot (left heel to right toe).

- **■ *Girl drag RF front LF***

Drag your right foot in front of the left foot (right heel to left toe).

Move 6 *count a*

- **■ *Boy RF side***

Step sideways and a little back with the right foot turning the toe out.

- **■ *Girl LF side***

Step sideways and a little back with the left foot turning the toe out.

Move 7 *count 2*

- **■ *Boy drag LF front RF***

Drag your left foot in front of the right foot (left heel to right toe).

- **■ *Girl drag RF front LF***

Drag your right foot in front of the left foot (right heel to left toe).

Volta travelling right

As with the volta left, the volta travelling right also has a gradual turn but this time, as the name suggests, turns up to three eighths of a turn to the right. The timing for this figure is: 1 a 2 a 1 a 2.

Move 1 *count 1*

■ *Boy RF front LF*

With your body BW and your weight on the left foot, start a turn to the right, place the right foot (heel to toe) in front of the left foot (right heel to left toe).

■ *Girl LF front RF*

With your body FW and your weight on the right foot, start a turn to the right, place the left foot (heel to toe) in front of the right foot (left heel to right toe).

Move 2 *count a*

■ *Boy LF side*

Step sideways and a little back with the left foot, turning the toe out.

■ *Girl RF side*

Step sideways and a little back with the right foot, turning the toe out.

Move 3 *count 2*

■ *Boy drag RF front LF*

Drag your right foot in front of the left foot (right heel to left toe).

■ *Girl drag LF front RF*

Drag your left foot in front of the right foot (right heel to left toe).

> **Note:** Again the next four moves are simply repeats of moves 2 and 3 as follows.

Move 4 *count a*

■ *Boy LF side*

Step sideways and a little back with the left foot, turning the toe out.

■ *Girl RF side*

Step sideways and a little back with the right foot, turning the toe out.

Move 5 *count 1*

■ *Boy drag RF front LF*

Drag your right foot in front of the left foot (right heel to left toe).

■ *Girl drag LF front RF*

Drag your left foot in front of the right foot (left heel to right toe).

Move 6 *count a*

■ *Boy LF side*

Step sideways and a little back with the left foot, turning the toe out.

■ *Girl RF side*

Step sideways and a little back with the right foot, turning the toe out.

Move 7 *count 2*

■ *Boy drag RF front LF*

Drag your right foot in front of the left foot (right heel to left toe).

■ *Girl drag LF front RF*

Drag your left foot in front of the right foot (left heel to right toe).

> **Note:** To put some of this together you can start with a volta travelling left then a volta travelling right followed by a whisk to the left.

Bota fogos

Bota fogos steps are a heap of fun to do and have the funkiest name that, believe it or not, is a real place in Brazil. Botafogo is pronounced 'boat a foe go', and it's the name of a neighbourhood in the city of Rio de Janeiro. Dance-wise, bota fogos are yet another classic step used in the samba and you'll recognize the steps the moment you attempt to dance it. Carmen Miranda wore this step out! We are going to learn two ways to do the bota fogos: first, bota fogos to PP and counter promenade position (CPP) and second, the travelling bota fogos.

Bota fogos to promenade position (PP) and counter promenade position (CPP)

There are nine steps in this figure, and the rhythm is: 1 a 2, 1 a 2, 1 a 2.

You use the ABB.

Move 1 *count 1*
■ *Boy LF forward*
With your body FW and your weight on the right foot take a step forwards with the left foot.

■ *Girl RF back*
With your body BW and your weight on the left foot take a step backwards with the right foot.

move 1

Move 2 *count a*

■ *Boy RF side*

Step sideways onto the right foot, with a little bit of weight as you start turning to the left.

■ *Girl LF side*

Step sideways onto the left foot, with a little bit of weight as you start turning to the right.

move 2

move 3

Move 3 *count 2*

■ *Boy weight onto LF*

Transfer your weight onto the left foot in PP as you continue the turn.

■ *Girl weight onto RF*

Transfer your weight onto the right foot in PP as you continue the turn.

> **Note:** During moves 2 and 3 you should have both completed one-eighth of a turn.

Move 4 *count 1*

■ *Boy RF forward*

Step forwards and across with the right foot in PP.

■ *Girl LF forward*

Step forwards and across with the left foot in PP.

move 4

move 5

Move 5 *count a*

■ *Boy LF side*

Step sideways with the left foot, placing a little weight on it as you start to turn to the right.

■ *Girl RF side*

Step sideways with the right foot, placing a little weight on it as you start to turn to the left.

Move 6 *count 2*

■ *Boy weight to RF*
Keeping the turn going, transfer your weight onto the right foot in CPP (girl on the boy's left side).

■ *Girl weight to LF*
Keeping the turn going, transfer your weight onto the left foot in CPP (girl on the boy's left side).

Move 7 *count 1*

> **Note:** You should have both now completed a quarter turn.

■ *Boy LF forward*
Step forwards and across with the left foot in PP.

■ *Girl RF forward*
Step forwards and across with the right foot in PP.

Move 8 *count a*

■ *Boy RF side*
Step sideways with your right foot, placing a little weight on it as you start to turn to the left.

■ *Girl LF side*
Step sideways with your left foot, placing a little weight on it as you start to turn to the right.

move 6

Move 9 *count 2*

■ *Boy weight to LF*
Transfer your weight onto the left foot in PP, continuing to turn to the left.

■ *Girl weight to RF*
Transfer your weight onto the right foot in PP, continuing to turn to the right.

> **Note:** You should have both now completed three-eighths of a turn. Follow with a RF samba walk in PP (girl LF).

Travelling bota fogos

The travelling bota fogos also have nine steps and the rhythm goes like this: 1 a 2, 1 a 2, 1 a 2.

Move 1 *count 1*

■ *Boy LF forward*

Start with your body facing DW outside your partner (on her left side) with your weight on the right foot, then step forwards with the left foot as you start to turn to the left.

■ *Girl RF back*

Start with your body backing DW with your weight on the left foot, then step backwards with the right foot as you start to turn to the left.

Move 2 *count a*

■ *Boy RF side*

Step sideways with the right foot, placing a little weight onto it as you continue to turn to the left.

■ *Girl LF side*

Step sideways with the left foot, placing a little weight onto it as you continue to turn to the left.

Move 3 *count 2*

■ *Boy weight onto LF*

Transfer your weight onto the left foot, finishing the turn.

■ *Girl weight onto RF*

Transfer your weight onto the right foot, finishing the turn.

> **Note:** You should have both now successfully completed a quarter of a turn.

Move 4 *count 1*

■ *Boy RF forward outside*

Step forwards with the right foot on the outside of your partner (on her right side) and start your turn to the right.

■ *Girl LF back*

Step backwards with the left foot as you start to turn to the right.

Move 5 *count a*

■ *Boy LF side*

Step sideways with the left foot, placing a little weight on it as you continue the turn.

■ *Girl RF side*

Step sideways with the right foot, placing a little weight on it as you continue to turn.

Move 6 *count 2*

■ *Boy weight onto RF*

Transfer your weight onto the right foot, completing the turn to the right.

■ *Girl weight onto LF*

Transfer your weight onto the left foot, completing the turn to the right.

> **Note:** You should have both now completed a quarter turn to the right.

Move 7 *count 1*

■ *Boy LF forward*

Step forwards with the left foot as you start to turn to the left.

■ *Girl RF back*

Step backwards with the right foot as you start to turn to the left.

Move 8 *count a*

■ *Boy RF side*

Step sideways with the right foot, placing a little weight onto it as you continue to turn to the left.

■ *Girl LF side*

Step sideways with the left foot, placing a little weight onto it as you continue to turn to the left.

Move 9 count 2

■ **Boy weight onto LF**

Transfer your weight onto the left foot, finishing the turn.

■ **Girl weight onto RF**

Transfer your weight onto the right foot, finishing the turn.

> **Note:** You should have both now successfully completed a quarter of a turn. You can then follow this with a natural basic, but boys take the first step outside your partner, ready to turn to face one another on move 2.

Corta jaca

'Corta jaca' is reputed to mean 'the cutting of the apple'. I can only guess this is because it cuts the floor fantastically. I really like this move and hope that you will too.

Start with a normal hold, and note that there is no bounce in this particular figure and the rhythm is different to all the other figures we've learnt to date. The timing for the corta jaca is even: 1, 2 and 1 and 2 and.

It's normally taught in Slows and Quicks but I've taken the liberty to keep it all in numerical counts to avoid a lonely waif and stray S and Q in the samba.

Move 1 count 1

■ **Boy RF forward**

Start by FW with your weight on the left foot, then take a strong and definite step forwards with the right foot.

■ **Girl LF back**

Start by BW with your weight on the right foot, then step backwards with the left foot.

Move 2 count 2

■ **Boy LF forward**

Step a little to the side and forwards on the heel of the left foot.

■ **Girl RF back**

Step a little to the side and backwards on the ball of the right foot.

Move 3 count and

■ **Boy RF slides L**

With your foot flat to the floor, slide the right foot leftwards.

■ **Girl LF slides R**

With your foot flat to the floor, slide the left foot rightwards.

Move 4 count 1

■ **Boy LF back**

Step backwards and a little to the side with the left ball.

■ **Girl RF back**

Step forwards and a little to the side with the right heel.

Move 5 count and

■ **Boy RF slides L**

With your foot flat to the floor, slide the right foot leftwards.

■ **Girl LF slides R**

With your foot flat to the floor, slide the left foot rightwards.

Move 6 *count 2*

■ *Boy LF forward*

Step a little to the side and forwards on the heel of the left foot.

■ *Girl RF back*

Step a little to the side and backwards on the ball of the right foot.

Move 7 *count and*

■ *Boy RF slides L*

With your foot flat to the floor, slide the right foot leftwards.

■ *Girl LF slides R*

With your foot flat to the floor, slide the left foot rightwards.

> **Note:** You can now try a progressive basic into the corta jaca and then thrill yourselves by doing a whisk to the left. This can be repeated.

Reverse turn

The reverse turn is a travelling step and it has six moves, the timing goes like this: 1 a 2, 1 a 2.

Start this figure in a normal hold and use the ABB.

Move 1 *count 1*

■ *Boy LF forward*

With your body facing the LOD and your weight on the right foot, step forwards with the left foot and start to turn to the left.

■ *Girl RF back*

With your body backing the LOD and your weight on the left foot, step backwards with the right foot as you start a turn to the left.

Move 2 *count a*

■ *Boy RF side*

Continuing the turn, step to the side and slightly back with the right foot.

■ *Girl LF closes to RF*

Place your left heel close to your right heel as you continue to turn to the left.

Move 3 *count 2*

■ *Boy LF crosses front RF*

Cross your left foot in front of the right foot with the toe turned out as you continue to turn to the left.

■ *Girl RF closes to LF*

Close your right foot to the left foot as you continue to turn to the left.

Move 4 *count 1*

■ *Boy RF back*

Take your right foot back and a little to the right as you continue the turn to the left.

■ *Girl LF forward*

Step forwards onto the left foot as you continue to turn to the left.

Move 5 *count a*

■ *Boy LF closes to RF*

Place your left heel close to the right heel as you continue to turn to the left.

■ *Girl RF side*

Take your right foot sideways and a little to the back as you continue to turn to the left.

Move 6 *count 2*

■ *Boy RF closes to LF*

Close your right foot to the left foot as you continue to turn left.

■ *Girl LF crosses front RF*

Cross your left foot in front of the right foot with the toe turned out as you continue to turn to the left.

Note: If you want to be dare-devilish, you can repeat this figure entirely, doubling it, taking the move number to 12. Follow the whole thing with the bota fogos to PP and CPP!

amalgamations

Amalgamations for the samba

Routine one

Natural basic

Whisk to right

Whisk to left

Whisk to right

Samba walks × 2

Whisk to left

Whisk to right

Whisk to left

Routine two

Whisk to right

Travelling voltas left

Travelling voltas right

Whisk to left

Corta jaca

Whisk to left

Routine three

Reverse turn

Bota fogos to PP and CPP

Bota fogos to PP

A further bota fogo (turning to end facing LOD for the boy and backing LOD for the girl)

All of the above can be repeated!

Make up your own!

....

....

....

....

....

....

....

cha cha cha

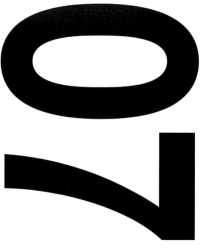

20 cha cha cha

A little bit of funky history

The cha cha cha is a Latin dance from Cuba. It's based on the rhythm of the triple mambo, consisting of two slow steps and three quick steps hence the rhythm 'slow slow cha cha cha' or 'cha cha cha slow slow'. The very words have a suggestion of bongo beats going mad, tantalizing timbales with maracas shaking the house down. The dance was originally an alternative form of the mambo and rumba, and it's said that a guy called Enrique Jorrin mixed the rhythms up creating this exciting new beat. Jorrin was born in Cuba in 1929 and became a big band leader in New York and, as one story goes, he was watching the dancers and noticed the sounds their feet made; they produced a 'shar-shar' noise as they moved across the ballroom floor. Inspired, Jorrin returned the next night with a brand new rhythm, which he tried out on the dancers. The response was extraordinary and, in the early 1950s, the cha cha cha took the world by storm. The dancers couldn't get enough of it and wanted more. The rhythm was so infectious, and the ease at which it could be adapted musically for very small bands or big bands made it accessible to almost everyone.

What music do I dance to?

The time signature for the cha cha cha is 4/4. That means four beats to every bar of music. You should be very familiar with this time signature if you have studied the rumba first. If you haven't, do it now, because you'll need good hip action for this dance and the rumba is slower than the cha cha cha so it is the best dance to get you ready and prepared! If this time signature doesn't freak you out and you already have good hip action, then the difference is that the fourth beat of the bar is split into half beats. You would then count like this: 2 3 4 and 1.

The 4 and 1 represent the cha cha cha rhythm. The tempo is set between 30–4 bars per minute, which is only slightly faster than the rumba, but the amount of steps in the cha cha cha make it feel much faster.

Track list

21 My introduction – getting you started

22 *Picture of You*

23 *Hot Stuff*

Have a listen now to track **21** to hear those famous cha cha cha rhythms.

The hold

The hold is the same as for the rumba and samba but you'll see that some of the sequences, like the time steps, can have no hold at all. The girls are a lot more active in this dance as they move to and from their partner and do turns under the arm of the boy.

The boy's job is to lead and support the girl, but he also gets to have a bit of fun with some hip action. It's important to keep the steps small because of the speed of the dance and remember that the footwork required for this particular dance is always ball to flat foot. In this dance you need to be really definite and precise with your leg and footwork. A good tip for the beginner is, when taking a step backwards on the ball of your foot, be very careful not to lower the heel too fast. This is a common error that most people make. Rhythm-wise, you need to let the last beat linger for a little like this: 'cha cha chaaa', the last beat having a longer value of time. Cha cha cha is a non-progressive dance, which means it pretty much stays on the spot and doesn't go hurtling around the dance floor.

Len's top tip

If dancing the cha cha cha
Go on to the floor like a star
You can bump, you can grind
And move your behind
One tip girls – best wear a bra!

The steps

Right foot and left foot cha cha cha chassé

This is the very first thing you'll need to get right because it is the basic movement that all the other steps stem from. The third step is held for a moment and you could think of it as 'cha cha hold' or, as described before 'cha

cha chaaa', whatever you find easiest to maintain the rhythm. You can practise this movement and rhythm on the spot by stepping three times and holding the last step. Give it a go now! Start with any foot and step step step (hold), then repeat on the other foot, step step step (hold). Just keep that going until you become familiar with the rhythm in your body and with how it feels. It should feel good, if it doesn't, perhaps you are doing something wrong like trying to step on the same foot twice. Keep it alternating with definite weight changes.

The chassé may be taken with or without turn in any forward, backward or sideways direction and also on the spot or 'in place'.

On the CD you'll hear me say a chassé as, 'side, close, side'.

The beat value for the cha cha cha chassé is:

- Count 4   = $1/2$ beat
- Count *and* = $1/2$ beat
- Count 1   = 1 whole beat.

Right foot cha cha cha chassé

For practice purposes counts 1, 2 and 3 are not danced.

Move 1 *count 4*
■ *Boy RF side*
With your feet apart, take a very small step to the side with the right foot.

■ *Girl LF side*
With your feet apart, take a very small step to the side with the left foot.

Move 2 *count and*
■ *Boy LF to RF*
Move your left foot a little towards the right foot.

■ *Girl RF to LF*
Move your right foot a little towards the left foot.

Move 3 *count 1*

■ *Boy RF side*
Take a small step to the side with the right foot.

■ *Girl LF side*
Take a small step to the side with the left foot.

Left foot cha cha cha chassé

Move 1 *count 4*

■ *Boy LF side*
Take a very small step to the side with the left foot.

■ *Girl RF side*
Take a very small step to the side with the right foot.

Move 2 *count and*

■ *Boy RF to LF*
Move your right foot a little to the left foot.

■ *Girl LF to RF*
Move your left foot a little to the right foot.

Move 3 *count 1*

■ *Boy LF side*
Take a really small step to the side with the left foot.

■ *Girl RF side*
Take a really small step to the side with the right foot.

Basic movement in place

'In place' just means dancing on the spot without travelling anywhere around the room. This whole figure is the decathlon of cha cha cha, meaning it has ten moves or steps making up the basic movement, from which all other steps are derivatives.

Count 1

Not danced.

Move 1 *count 2*

■ *Boy step LF*
Take a step in place with the left foot.

■ *Girl step RF*
Take a step in place with the right foot.

Move 2 *count 3*

■ *Boy step RF*
Take a step in place with the right foot.

■ *Girl step LF*
Take a step in place with the left foot.

> **Note:** Moves 3–5 counts 4 and 1: you both do a cha cha cha chassé.

Move 3 *count 4*

■ *Boy LF side*
Take a very small step to the side with the left foot.

■ *Girl RF side*
Take a very small step to the side with the right foot.

Move 4 *count and*

■ *Boy RF to LF*
Move your right foot a little to the left foot.

■ *Girl LF to RF*
Move your left foot a little to the right foot.

Move 5 *count 1*

■ *Boy LF side*
Take a really small step to the side with the left foot.

■ *Girl RF side*
Take a really small step to the side with the right foot.

Move 6 *count 2*

■ *Boy RF to LF*
Move your right foot a little to the left foot (almost close).

■ *Girl LF to RF*
Move your left foot a little to the right foot (almost close).

Move 7 *count 3*

■ *Boy step LF*
Take a step in place with the left foot.

■ *Girl step RF*
Take a step in place with the right foot.

Note: Moves 8–10 counts 4 and 1: you both do another cha cha cha chassé.

Move 8 *count 4*

■ *Boy RF side*
Take a small step to the side with the right foot.

■ *Girl LF side*
Take a small step to the side with the left foot.

Move 9 *count and*

■ *Boy LF to RF*
Move your left foot a little to the right foot (almost close).

■ *Girl RF to LF*
Move your right foot a little to the left foot (almost close).

Move 10 *count 1*

■ *Boy RF side*
Take a very small step to the side with the right foot.

■ *Girl LF side*
Take a very small step to the side with the left foot.

Try it with tracks 22 and 23 on the CD!

Forward basic movement

If you are having difficulties with the rhythm and speed of it all, go back and try it again calmly, quietly and slowly, and then work up to it.

Listen to track **21** on the CD where I'll talk you through the forward and back basic movement and give you a good idea of the rhythms.

The forward and back basic have a total of ten steps and the rhythm goes like this: 2, 3, 4 and 1, 2, 3, 4 and 1.

The basic figure is made up of two parts, the first is the forward basic movement and the second is the back basic movement. It's possible to only dance a forward or a back at any one time, as you'll discover from the routines later on.

You should be in a normal hold with your feet apart, with the boy's weight on his right foot and the girl's weight on her left foot. You can start this figure facing any direction.

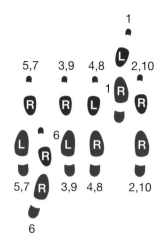

figure 19   forward and back basic

Count 1

Not danced.

Move 1 *count 2*

■ *Boy LF forward*

With your weight on the right foot, step forwards with the left foot.

■ *Girl RF back*

With your weight on the left foot, step backwards with the right foot.

move 1

move 2

Move 2 *count 3*

■ *Boy weight to RF*

Replace your weight back onto the right foot.

■ *Girl weight to LF*

Replace your weight forwards onto the left foot.

> **Note:** The timing for the chassés that follow are as in the ten move basic described on pages 152–3.

Moves 3–5 *counts 4 and 1*

■ *Boy LF side chassé LRL*

Move your left foot sideways and chassé left, right, left.

■ *Girl RF side chassé RLR*

Move your right foot sideways and chassé right, left, right.

Now carry on with the second part, the back basic movement.

move 3

move 4

move 5

Back basic movement

Move 6 *count 2*

■ *Boy RF back*
Step backwards with the right foot.

■ *Girl LF forward*
Step forwards with the left foot.

move 6

move 7

Move 7 *count 3*

■ *Boy weight to LF*
Replace your weight forwards onto the left foot.

■ *Girl weight to RF*
Replace your weight back onto the right foot.

Moves 8–10 *counts 4 and 1*

■ *Boy RF side chassé RLR*

Move your right foot sideways and chassé right, left, right.

■ *Girl LF side chassé LRL*

Move your left foot sideways and chassé left, right, left.

Be brave! Go and dance the steps to some music. Try track 23.

move 8

move 9

move 10

Basic movement turning left

You should be in a normal hold with your feet apart and the boy's weight on his right foot and the girl's weight on her left foot. You can start this figure facing any direction but if you would like a position to begin in, the boy could be FW with the girl BW. This will help you to know when you have achieved a complete full turn to the left.

This figure consists of ten steps and the rhythm goes like this: 2, 3, 4 and 1, 2, 3, 4 and 1.

Count 1

Not danced.

Move 1 *count 2*

■ *Boy LF forward*

With your weight on the right foot step forwards with the left foot as you start to turn to the left.

■ *Girl RF back*

With your weight on the left foot step backwards with the right foot as you start to turn to the left.

Move 2 *count 3*

■ *Boy weight to RF*

As you continue the turn, replace your weight back onto the right foot.

■ *Girl weight to LF*

As you continue the turn, replace your weight forwards onto the left foot.

> **Note:** The timing for the chassés that follow are as in the ten move basic described on pages 152–3.

Moves 3–5 *counts 4 and 1*

■ *Boy LF side chassé LRL*

Move your left foot sideways and a little back and chassé left, right, left, while continuing to turn to the left.

■ *Girl RF side chassé RLR*

Move your right foot sideways and a little forward and chassé right, left, right, while continuing to turn to the left.

Move 6 *count 2*

■ *Boy RF back*

As you continue to turn left, step backwards with the right foot.

■ *Girl LF forward*

As you continue to turn left, step forwards with the left foot.

Move 7 *count 3*

■ *Boy weight to LF*

As you continue to turn, replace your weight forwards onto the left foot.

■ *Girl weight to RF*

As you continue to turn, replace your weight back onto the right foot.

Moves 8–10 *counts 4 and 1*

■ *Boy RF side chassé RLR*

Move your right foot sideways and a little forward and chassé right, left, right, while continuing to turn to the left to finish FW.

■ *Girl LF side chassé LRL*

Move your left foot sideways and a little back and chassé left, right, left, while continuing to turn to the left to finish BW.

Three cha cha chas

You'll really love this particular move as it can fly, and your feet are getting a good workout. It's really simple and enormously satisfying to dance.

The step is simply three chassés in a row danced continuously in one direction. It can be danced forwards, or backwards and side by side. As you have been dancing your chassés on the count of four, let's begin there. The timing is: 4 and 1 – 2 and 3 – 4 and 1.

So you see, you just do an extra chassé in the middle on counts 2 and 3; it couldn't be easier.

> **Note:** If you want to dance a forward chassé followed by a backward chassé, then you must dance steps 1–2 of a basic forward movement (for the boy) or back movement (for the girl) in order to link the two moves together.
>
> You can use normal position, open facing position with no hold or left to right hand hold, low double hand hold alternating the hands. If you want to get more adventurous, you could substitute your chassés for locks.

New York in the cha cha cha

You will have noticed that there are a lot of steps in the cha cha cha that are the same as in the rumba. It's just the rhythm that changes slightly as it has a cha cha cha chassé on every third step. The New York is a standard figure in Latin dancing and there are many variations. The one you are about to learn comes directly out of a basic movement, which you've just been practising. When you get to the end of the basic movement, you'll need to release your hold with the right hand in order to get into the left S×S position. This figure has ten steps and the rhythm goes like this: 2, 3, 4 and 1, 2, 3, 4 and 1. Get ready now and let's begin!

Start in a normal or double hand hold with feet slightly apart.

Count 1

Not danced.

Move 1 *count 2*

- **Boy LF forward turn R**

Facing your partner with your weight on the right foot, release hold of the right hand and make a quarter of a turn to the right while moving forwards with your left foot, to end in the left S×S position.

- **Girl RF forward turn L**

Facing your partner with your weight on the left foot, release hold of the left hand and make a quarter of a turn to the left while moving forwards with your right foot, to end in the left S×S position.

Move 2 *count 3*

- **Boy weight to RF**

Transfer your weight back onto the right foot.

- **Girl weight to LF**

Transfer your weight back onto the left foot.

Moves 3–5 *counts 4 and 1*

- **Boy LF side chassé LRL**

Step sideways with your left foot and chassé left, right, left. You'll also be turning a quarter to the left with your body FW and looking at your partner, regaining hold. If you are looking at the back of her head something has gone horribly wrong!

- **Girl RF side chassé RLR**

Step sideways with your right foot and chassé right, left, right. You will be turning a quarter to the right with your body FC, ending up face to face with your partner, regaining hold.

Move 6 *count 2*

■ *Boy RF forward*

Release hold of the left hand and make a quarter of a turn to the left while moving forwards with your right foot, to end in the right SxS position.

■ *Girl LF forward*

Release hold of the right hand and make a quarter of a turn to the right while moving forwards with your left foot, to end in the right SxS position.

Move 7 *count 3*

■ *Boy weight to LF*

Transfer weight back to the left foot.

■ *Girl weight to RF*

Transfer weight back to the right foot.

Moves 8–10 *counts 4 and 1*

This is simply a repeat of moves 3–5 but on the opposite feet.

■ *Boy RF side chassé RLR*

Step sideways with your right foot and chassé right, left, right. You'll also be turning to the right with your body FW and looking at your partner, regaining hold.

■ *Girl LF side chassé LRL*

Step sideways with your left foot and chassé left, right, left. You will be turning in opposition to your partner leftwards, ending FC, regaining hold and face to face with your beau!

Why don't you try and syncopate your New York?

There's so much fun to be had in trying! This will make you look as though you've been training for years. It's totally hip and funky but, be warned, it's unbelievably fast. Practise it well before showing anyone (you don't want to be ridiculed by your so-called friends) – with rehearsal, you'll go on to surprise and thrill with this divine deviation!

To dance the syncopated New York, the rhythm is: 2 and 3 – 4 and 1.

Basically this is a double cha cha cha rhythm.

Count 1

Not danced.

Move 1 *count 2*

■ *Boy LF forward*

Take an eighth turn to the right as you step forwards onto the left foot.

■ *Girl RF forward*

Take an eighth turn to the left as you step forwards onto the right foot.

Move 2 *count and*

■ *Boy weight to RF*

Transfer your weight onto the right foot before turning to face your partner.

■ *Girl weight to LF*

Transfer your weight onto the left foot before turning to face your partner.

Move 3 *count 3*

■ *Boy LF side*

Step sideways with the left foot.

■ *Girl RF side*

Step sideways with the right foot.

Move 4 *count 4*

■ *Boy RF forward*

Take an eighth turn to the left as you step forwards onto the right foot.

■ *Girl LF forward*

Take an eighth turn to the right as you step forwards onto the left foot.

Move 5 *count and*

■ *Boy weight to LF*

Transfer your weight onto the left foot before turning to face your partner.

■ *Girl weight to RF*

Transfer your weight onto the right foot before turning to face your partner.

Move 6 *count 1*

■ *Boy RF side*

Step sideways with the right foot.

■ *Girl LF side*

Step sideways with the left foot.

Spot turns

Spot turns take place on the spot, hence the name. You can dance them individually or together and they can go left or right. They're the same for the boy and the girl but if you dance them at the same time, you need to do the turns in opposite directions; one turning to the left, and one turning to the right.

This figure has five moves and the rhythm goes like this: 2, 3, 4 and 1.

Count 1

Not danced.

Move 1 *count 2*

■ ■ *LF forward*

Start with your feet apart and your weight on the right foot and no hold, then move your left foot forwards as you start to turn to the right.

Move 2 *count 3*

■ ■ *weight to RF*

Transfer your weight forwards onto the right foot as you continue to turn.

Moves 3–5 *counts 4 and 1*

■ ■ *R chassé side LRL*

Keep the turn going as you chassé sideways left, right, left. You should have completed one whole turn ending back facing your partner.

Now let's try a spot turn to the left.

Count 1

Not danced.

Move 1 *count 2*

■ ■ *RF forward*

Start with your feet apart and your weight on the left foot and no hold, then move your right foot forwards as you start to turn to the left.

Move 2 *count 3*

■ ■ *weight to LF*

Transfer your weight forwards onto the left foot as you continue to turn.

Moves 3–5 *counts 4 and 1*

■ ■ *L chassé side RLR*

Keep the turn going as you chassé sideways right, left, right. You should have completed one whole turn ending back facing your partner.

Hand to hand in the cha cha cha

Why not now have a go at the good old hand to hand that you learnt in the rumba? The only difference here is the addition of the chassés.

This figure consists of ten steps and the rhythm goes like this: 2, 3, 4 and 1, 2, 3, 4 and 1.

Start this move in a double hand hold.

Count 1

Not danced.

Move 1 *count 2*

■ *Boy LF back R SxS*

Facing your partner with your weight on the right foot, release hold of the left hand and make a quarter of a turn to the left while stepping backwards with the left foot to end in right SxS position.

■ *Girl RF back R SxS*

Facing your partner with your weight on the left foot, release hold of the right hand and make a quarter of a turn to the right while stepping backwards with the right foot to end in right SxS position.

Move 2 *count 3*

■ *Boy weight to RF*

Transfer your weight onto the right foot.

■ *Girl weight to LF*

Transfer your weight onto the left foot.

Moves 3–5 *counts 4 and 1*

■ *Boy LF side chassé LRL*

Step sideways with the left foot as you turn a quarter turn to the right to face your partner, regaining the double hand hold as you chassé left, right, left.

■ *Girl RF side chassé RLR*

Step sideways with your right foot as you turn a quarter turn to the left to face your partner, regaining the double hand hold as you chassé right, left, right.

Move 6 *count 2*

■ *Boy RF back L S×S*

Release hold of the right hand and make a quarter of a turn to the right while stepping backwards with the right foot to end in left S×S position.

■ *Girl LF back L S×S*

Release hold of the left hand and make a quarter of a turn to the left while stepping backwards with the left foot to end in left S×S position.

Move 7 *count 3*

■ *Boy weight to LF*

Transfer your weight onto the left foot.

■ *Girl weight to RF*

Transfer your weight onto the right foot.

Moves 8–10 *counts 4 and 1*

■ *Boy RF side chassé RLR*

Step sideways with the right foot as you turn a quarter turn to the left, regaining the double hand hold and gazing into your partner's eyes, and chassé right, left, right.

■ *Girl LF side chassé LRL*

You should know by now what this is. Yes, you're correct! You step sideways with the left foot as you turn a quarter turn to the right, regaining the double hand hold, and chassé left, right, left, ending up in the same position as the boy, gazing, gazing, gazing.

If you fancy, you can go right ahead and repeat this or follow it with a back basic: the decision is entirely yours.

Time steps

Time steps are great to mark time if your partner forgets the routine or selfishly starts improvising and doing their own steps. If this happens to you, you can save yourself and keep your dignity by dancing a holding pattern until your partner comes back to their senses. This holding pattern is called a 'time step'.

It depends what routine you're doing to know if you should start this move on the left or right as it can begin on either. You can start it in a normal hold or an open

facing position, with hold or without hold. See, fabulously versatile!

Left foot time step

Note: Just to confuse the ladies, while the man dances a left foot time step, you dance a right foot time step and when the man dances a right foot time step, you dance a left foot time step. As you can see, the lefts and rights are taken from the boy's perspective.

The left foot time step has five moves and the rhythm goes like this: 2, 3, 4 and 1.

Count 1

Not danced.

Move 1 *count 2*

■ *Boy LF behind*

Start with feet apart and your weight on the right foot, then step behind your right foot with the left foot, turning the toe out a little.

■ *Girl RF behind*

Start with feet apart and your weight on the left foot, then step behind your left foot with the right foot, turning the toe out a little.

Move 2 *count 3*

■ *Boy weight to RF*

Transfer your weight onto the right foot.

■ *Girl weight to LF*

Transfer your weight onto the left foot.

Moves 3–5 *counts 4 and 1*

■ *Boy LF side chassé LRL*

Step sideways with the left foot and chassé, facing your partner left, right, left.

■ *Girl RF side chassé RLR*

Step sideways with the right foot and chassé, facing your partner right, left, right.

Right foot time step

The right foot time step has five moves and the rhythm goes like this: 2, 3, 4 and 1.

Count 1

Not danced.

Move 1 *count 2*
- **Boy RF behind**

Start with feet apart and your weight on the left foot, then step behind your left foot with the right foot, turning the toe out a little.

- **Girl LF behind**

Start with feet apart and your weight on the right foot, then step behind your right foot with the left foot, turning the toe out a little.

Move 2 *count 3*
- **Boy weight to LF**

Transfer your weight onto the left foot.

- **Girl weight to RF**

Transfer your weight onto the right foot.

Moves 3–5 *counts 4 and 1*
- **Boy RF side chassé RLR**

Step sideways with the right foot and chassé, facing your partner right, left, right.

- **Girl LF side chassé LRL**

Step sideways with the left foot and chassé, facing your partner left, right, left.

> **Note:** You can dance a left foot time step followed by a right foot time step and repeat it. You can also mix and match with a spot turn – while either partner is dancing a right foot time step, the other half can dance a spot turn to the right or, if one is dancing a left foot time step, the other can dance a spot turn to the left. Isn't that fierce?

The fan in the cha cha cha

You should know this already from the rumba, but this is its cha cha cha incarnation. Start by dancing the first five moves of the forward basic then follow this with the fan. This whole figure consists of ten moves in total and the rhythm goes like this: 2, 3, 4 and 1, 2, 3, 4 and 1.

Count 1

Not danced.

Move 1 *count 2*
- **Boy LF forward**

With your weight on the right foot, step forwards with the left foot.

- **Girl RF back**

With your weight on the left foot, step backwards with the right foot.

Move 2 *count 3*
- **Boy weight to RF**

Transfer your weight back onto the right foot.

- **Girl weight to LF**

Transfer your weight back onto the left foot.

Moves 3–5 *counts 4 and 1*
- **Boy LF side chassé LRL**

Move your left foot sideways and a little back and chassé left, right, left.

- **Girl RF side chassé RLR**

Move your right foot sideways and chassé right, left, right.

The Fan

Move 6 *count 2*

- **Boy RF back**

Step back onto the right foot, leaving the left foot in place. At the same time, you need to lead your partner forwards towards you.

- **Girl LF forward**

Step forwards onto the left foot in between your partner's feet.

Move 7 *count 3*

- **Boy LF forward**

Transfer your weight forwards onto the left foot as you release the hold with the right hand.

- **Girl RF back**

Step backwards with the right foot at right angles to your partner as you start to turn to the left.

Moves 8–10 *counts 4 and 1*

- **Boy RF side chassé RLR**

Step sideways with your right foot and chassé right, left, right. Extend your left arm to waist height as your partner pulls away from you.

- **Girl LF back chassé LRL**

Step back with your left foot and chassé left, right, left remaining at right angles to your partner to end in the fan position.

The hockey stick in the cha cha cha

The hockey stick in the cha cha cha is almost the same as the hockey stick in the rumba except for the addition of cha cha cha chassés on counts 4 and 1. Now go and cha cha cha your way into hockeystick heaven by trying this little winner! It has ten glorious steps and the rhythm goes like this: 2, 3, 4 and 1, 2, 3, 4 and 1.

Count 1

Not danced.

Move 1 *count 2*

- **Boy LF forward**

From the fan position, step forwards onto the left foot, leaving the right foot in place.

- **Girl RF closes to LF**

From the fan position, close your right foot to your left foot.

Move 2 *count 3*

- **Boy weight to RF**

Transfer weight back onto your right foot, leaving the left foot in place. Start to bring your partner towards you.

- **Girl LF forward**

Walk forwards on to the LF.

Moves 3–5 *counts 4 and 1*

- **Boy LF closes to RF**

Step sideways with your left foot and chassé left, right, left, almost on the spot, continuing to lead your partner towards you. At this point you need to make a hand adjustment so you don't break each other's wrists.

Note: The boy starts the move with the palm of his left hand facing skywards as he brings the girl into him on move 2. On move 3 he raises his left arm and, at the same time, rotates his hand towards himself to accommodate the girl (as you would if shielding your eyes from the sun), and then away from himself to end in a normal palm to palm hold with the thumb down.

- *Girl RF forward*

Walk forwards onto the right foot and chassé right, left, right.

Move 6 *count 2*

- *Boy RF back*

Take a small step back onto the right foot as you turn a bit to the right, leading your partner past you, raising your hand above her head.

- *Girl LF forward turn L*

Walk forwards onto the left foot and start to turn to the the in front of your partner.

Move 7 *count 3*

- *Boy weight to LF*

Transfer your weight forwards onto the left foot, leading your partner forwards away from you.

- *Girl RF forward turn L*

As you continue the turn to the left, step forwards onto the right foot, turning in towards your partner.

> **Note:** This forward step for the girl is the part of the hockey stick shape that curves at the end of the stick, hence the name!

Moves 8–10 *counts 4 and 1*

- *Boy RF forward*

Step forwards on your right foot and chassé right, left, right to end in an open facing position. On completion of your partner's step lower your left hand to waist height.

- *Girl LF back*

Step backwards on your left foot and chassé back, left, right, left to end facing your partner.

The Alemana turn in the cha cha cha

You've danced this move before in the rumba (remember the move where the girl is spun around under the boy's arm?). The difference is in the timing. Do a forward basic movement (see page 154) before this then take a look at how it goes in the cha cha cha. There are ten steps and the rhythm goes like this: 2, 3, 4 and 1, 2, 3, 4 and 1.

Count 1

Not danced.

Move 1 *count 2*

- *Boy LF forward*

With your weight on the right foot, step forwards with the left foot.

- *Girl RF back*

With your weight on the left foot, step backwards with the right foot.

Move 2 *count 3*

- *Boy weight to RF*

Transfer your weight onto the right foot.

- *Girl weight to LF*

Transfer your weight onto the left foot.

Moves 3–5 *counts 4 and 1*

- *Boy chassé LRL in place*

Take a very small step sideways with the left foot and chassé on the spot left, right, left.

- *Girl chassé RLR to side*

Step sideways with your right foot and chassé to the side right, left, right, as you start to turn to the right.

Move 6 *count 2*

■ *Boy RF back, release RH*

Step backwards with the right foot and lead your partner to turn right underneath your left arm. Don't forget to let go of your hold with your right hand otherwise you'll get all tangled up and the whole thing will be a disaster!

■ *Girl LF forward*

Step forwards with the left foot, continuing to turn.

Move 7 *count 3*

■ *Boy weight to LF*

Transfer your weight onto the left foot.

■ *Girl RF forward*

Step forwards with the right foot, continuing the turn.

Moves 8–10 *counts 4 and 1*

■ *Boy chassé side RLR*

Step sideways with the right foot and chassé right, left, right, then take up the normal hold.

■ *Girl chassé side LRL*

Completing the turn to the right, step sideways with the left foot and chassé left, right, left, ending up facing your partner and taking up the normal hold again.

Crack open the champagne, boys – your girl has just completed a full turn! You can follow this move with a basic or why not steam ahead and try a hand to hand? Try it with track **23** on the CD.

> **Note:** A little word of warning. If you dance this from an open facing position, as you will in the routine at the end of the chapter, then during moves 3–5 the girl needs to take the step forwards and not sideways.

Shoulder to shoulder

Sounds intimate, doesn't it? This is a variation that travels outside your partner, so if you've just completed a basic the boys will need to start thinking about stepping outside the girls in order to go into this move. You can also do a spot turn into it, so give that a go as well.

This figure has ten steps and the rhythm goes like this: 2, 3, 4 and 1, 2, 3, 4 and 1.

Count 1

Not danced.

Move 1 *count 2*

■ *Boy LF forward outside*

Step forwards onto the left foot, placing it outside your partner's left side.

■ *Girl RF back*

Step backwards onto the right foot.

Move 2 *count 3*

■ *Boy weight to RF*

Transfer your weight onto the right foot.

■ *Girl weight to LF*

Transfer your weight onto the left foot.

Moves 3–5 *counts 4 and 1*

■ *Boy LF side chassé LRL*

Step sideways with the left foot and chassé left, right, left, as you make a quarter turn to the left.

■ *Girl RF side chassé RLR*

Step sideways with the right foot and chassé right, left, right, as you make a quarter turn to the left.

Move 6 *count 2*

■ *Boy RF forward outside*

Step forwards with the right foot, placing it outside your partner's right side.

■ *Girl LF back*

Step backwards onto the left foot.

Move 7 *count 3*

■ *Boy weight to LF*

Transfer your weight onto the left foot.

■ *Girl weight to RF*

Transfer your weight onto the right foot.

Moves 8–10 *counts 4 and 1*

■ *Boy RF side chassé RLR*

Step sideways with your right foot and chassé right, left, right, while doing a quarter turn to the right.

■ *Girl LF side chassé LRL*

Step sideways with your left foot and chassé left, right, left, while doing a quarter turn to the right.

There and back step

You'll enjoy doing this one! See if it makes you laugh. It's difficult not to make it look camp, so guys, I wish you all the luck in the world.

This figure has ten steps and the rhythm goes like this: 1, 2, 3, 4 and 1, 2, 3, 4 and 1.

On moves 3–5, you both back away from each other, and on moves 8–10 you come back together.

Count 1

Not danced.

Move 1 *count 2*

■ *Boy LF forward*

Step forwards with the left foot, almost in place.

■ *Girl RF back*

Step backwards with the right foot, almost in place.

Move 2 *count 3*

■ *Boy weight to RF*

Transfer your weight onto the right foot.

■ *Girl weight to LF*

Transfer your weight onto the left foot.

Moves 3–5 *counts 4 and 1*

This is the camp bit. Boys, try and be butch!

■ *Boy LRL back*

Travel backwards with three small steps, left, right, left.

■ *Girl RLR back*

Travel backwards with three small steps, right, left, right.

Move 6 *count 2*

■ *Boy RF back*

Take a small step back with the right foot, almost in place.

■ *Girl LF forward*

Take a small step forwards with the left foot, almost in place.

Move 7 *count 3*

■ *Boy weight to LF*

Transfer your weight onto the left foot.

■ *Girl weight to RF*

Transfer your weight onto the right foot.

Moves 8–10 *counts 4 and 1*

■ *Boy RLR forward*

Travel forwards towards your partner by taking three small steps, right, left, right.

■ *Girl LRL forward*

Travel forwards towards your partner by taking three small steps, left, right, left.

I do hope you enjoyed that little bit of fun. You can also do this by dancing together in a normal hold where you move the same way. The girl just has to move forwards on moves 3–5 and backwards on moves 8–10.

Amalgamations for the cha cha cha

Routine one

Forward basic movement

Back basic movement

Repeat forward and back movements again

Left foot New York, right foot New York, left foot New York

Spot turn to the left for boy and right for girl

Routine two

Forward basic movement

Alemana turn

Right hand to hand

Spot turn to left for boy and right for girl

Shoulder to shoulder

Routine three

Forward basic

Fan

Hockey stick

Alemana turn

Right hand to hand

Spot turn to left for boy and right for girl

Time steps

make up your own

Make up your own!

....

....

....

....

....

....

....

....

jive

jive

A little bit of jovial jive history

It's the 1950s and jukeboxes are blaring, everyone is jiving, footloose and fancy-free. The Second World War is over and rock 'n' roll has well and truly kicked in. The jive was extreme and unbelievably physical, full of outrageous lifts, jumps and acrobatics! It was dangerous on a crowded dance floor, and was banned in public ballrooms; it could only be danced in controlled environments like competitive dancing. Jive was originally brought to the sunny shores of the UK by those wild and crazy American GIs during the Second World War. Jive was the trendy name back then for the 'lindy hop' which actually started in 1927 when a guy called Charles Lindbergh was the first pilot ever to fly non-stop across the Atlantic. A large heading in the newspapers read: 'Lindy Hops over the Atlantic'. People celebrated and with that a new dance was born and the original dance called the 'Hop', which had been around for years, became the Lindy Hop which eventually permeated the jive.

My One and Only, the hit show I choreographed in the West End in London, was set in 1927 and the story was all about a pilot trying to be the first to cross (hop) the Atlantic only to be beaten (because of love) by Charles Lindbergh. It was a great opportunity for me to use the excitement of the lindy hop and jitterbug as a base style

to some of the big dance sequences. The amazing athleticism and sheer energy of the dance provides entertainment and pure pleasure for the viewer. Dancing the dance is even more amazing, and you'll discover that just the basics will get you revved up and itching to throw yourself about.

The lindy hop wasn't the only dance that came into play; the jitterbug was the next big craze to hit the scene, and that was to the music of the great swing masters of 1937, including Benny Goodman, Cab Calloway and the incredible Duke Ellington. Teenagers were mad for it, and it kept changing in style with the trends, turning into American swing, West Coast swing, boogie woogie, among many other variations, until finally it was generically put together and called jive!

The jive is a non-progressive dance, which means that it doesn't move around the dance floor but stays pretty much in place. It can be danced in a very explosive way for competition, but you are about to learn a more relaxed and easy social dance that you'll be able to do anywhere. Naturally, if after acquiring the skills of the basic patterns you discover you have an uncontrollable hunger to learn more, you can do so (see the taking it further section on page 196).

What music do I dance to?

The time signature for the jive is 4/4, which means four beats to every bar of music, counted 1 2 3 4. Notice that the first and third beats are emphasized. You'll hear this in the drums, and it will help you to keep in time with the music. The big thing about the jive is the rhythm, and the first thing you need to do as a beginner is to get that rhythm into your body. In the jive you count like this: 1 2 3 a 4.

The tempo for the jive can be set at anything between 36–48 bars per minute. Be warned – this is another fast dance, so the more you practise together, the more able you'll be able to cope with the pace.

Track list

24 My introduction – getting you started.

25 *Soul Bossa Nova*

26 *Shake a Tail Feather*

The hold

The basic hold for the jive is a normal Latin dance hold, but a little more relaxed. You'll see that there are other holds that come into play, like the double hand hold (hand to hand), that you already know well from the cha cha cha. Like the cha cha cha, there are times when you will release the hold to do turns and other moves. If something feels even the slightest bit awkward when it comes to changing holds, you are possibly using the wrong hand or footwork, so always take the time to re-read the description to be certain that you've completely understood it. If you are getting confused about all the different holds, then go back to the photos of the holds on page 15 onwards to remind yourself. Don't rush, take all the time you need to practise the basics before going on to the harder stuff. With a good foundation and knowledge of the basics, you will feel confident and look great!

You really have to work together in this dance. In particular, the boy won't be able to shout out the steps that he anticipates doing, so instead he must 'talk with his hands'. By that I mean lead the girl well into the next step, otherwise she will look clueless and clumsy, and he won't be thanked for it! Communication is the key to a successful partnership.

How do I get the rhythm in my body and hands?

Very good question! Practise and listen to the music. Below is a small exercise that will help you to begin feeling the jive rhythm. You should be familiar with the word chassé as we have used it in the cha cha cha. If you skipped that section you should go back and study it because it will make the jive a whole lot easier and faster for you. If it has been a while since you did a cha cha cha chassé, then go back and glance at page 151 to remind yourselves.

The chassé in the jive is similar to the cha cha cha but the timing is different.

The first beat of the chassé has a syncopated feel, unlike the cha cha cha, which is even with two half beats and one whole beat during the chassé.

- Beat 1, count 3   = $^{3}/_{4}$ of a beat
- Count a   = $^{1}/_{4}$ of a beat
- Beat 2, count 4   = 1 whole beat.

It still has three steps, but it's counted in a different way. Those three steps can be taken sideways, backwards, forwards or even turning, and in any direction, be it left or right. The jive chassé is counted like this: 3 a 4. It's normal (in some ballroom circles) to do two in a row counting them like this: 3 a 4, 3 a 4.

Extremely important note: This can be our little secret: because there's a weird six count phrase through the basic jive, I secretly prefer to continue the counts to 5 a 6. So, if you were to count a whole six beat phrase, that phrase would go something like this: 1, 2, 3 a 4, 5 a 6.

It can be a little confusing to begin with because the main figure of the jive is really half a phrase short of filling the whole two bars of music (six beats instead of eight). You are left with two counts to fill and that's why there are link steps to fill those two counts. Don't panic! When you get familiar with it, you'll be dancing and not counting at all, and it will all become clear as you work through. Please don't skip any sections as each section leads you directly to the next.

A little exercise to get you in the mood

This is simply an exercise to help you feel the rhythm of the jive. It is slow, and you'll say to yourself: side, side, back, replace. The timing goes like this: 1–2, 3–4, 5, 6.

- Counts 1–2 = Side (Slow)
- Counts 3–4 = Side (Slow)
- Count 5 = Back (Quick)
- Count 6 = Replace (Quick).

As you can see, this adds up to a total of six beats and is counted over $1\frac{1}{2}$ bars of music. Now let's try our first go at the jive rhythm. This will eventually tie in with the steps you'll be doing later.

You can both practise on the same foot and use all small steps. Pretend you are holding your partner hand to hand in a double hand hold.

Side Take a step to the side with your left foot in a sort of rocking motion, then stay there for counts 1 and 2, leaving your right foot in place.

Your hands should move with the rocking motion, left hand down as right hand goes up slightly.

Side Take a step to the other side with your right foot, placing your weight on it for counts 3–4, leaving your left foot in place.

Your hands should do the reverse, as the right hand goes back down, the left hand goes slightly up.

Back Take a step backwards with your left foot, placing it behind the right foot (left toe behind the right heel) on count 5.

When you are in a hold together you will feel a slight pull on the hands as your bodies open out a little on this back step.

Replace Replace or (transfer) your weight forwards on to your right foot on count 6.

> **Note:** To help you get the rhythm, as you dance say, 'rock, rock, back, step'.

Repeat all of this until you've got it, then try getting together and doing it. When you work as partners, the girl will start on the opposite foot, otherwise you'll be dancing at the opposite ends of the room.

If you feel confident now, move on up the ladder and try the jive chassé.

> **Len's top tip**
>
> This dance is fast and alive
> Keep cool if you want to survive
> There's kicks and there's flicks
> And plenty of tricks
> One warning, don't drink and jive!

The steps

Jive chassés left and right

Let's get your jive chassés sorted out first and when you've mastered them you can begin to speed them up. You should feel a small little pause or held moment on moves 3 and 6 and go for a real change of weight when you hit the back step.

Chassé to the left

Counts 1, 2
Not danced.

(for the boy or girl)
Move 1 *count 3*
■ ■ *LF side*
Take a small step sideways with the left foot.

Move 2 *count a*
■ ■ *RF close towards LF*
Close your right foot towards the left foot.

Move 3 *count 4*
■ ■ *LF side*
Take a small step sideways with the left foot.

Chassé to the right

Move 4 *count 5*
■ ■ *RF side*
Take a small step sideways with the right foot.

Move 5 *count a*
■ ■ *LF close towards RF*
Close your left foot towards the right foot.

Move 6 *count 6*
■ ■ *RF side*
Take a small step sideways with the right foot.

Try and increase the tempo of this section to get you up to speed before you carry on. If you're thrilled with your level of attainment and the speed at which you're progressing, go on to the fallaway rock!

Fallaway rock

A fallaway is a V-shaped dance position similar to PP, but with the boy and girl moving backwards! If you want to take a peek at page 17 you'll see it demonstrated. Think of it as falling away from your partner slightly but staying connected – there will be a slight pull on the hand that is leading (joined with your partner).

The fallaway rock is your basic jive pattern and you'll need to practise this endlessly if you really want to move on. This figure will instill in you the fabulous jive rhythm. It's a classic, so fall away and rock!

This figure has eight moves and the rhythm goes like this: 1, 2, 3 a 4, 5 a 6.

Listen to track 24 where I will talk you through the fallaway rock.

Start this figure in a normal hold.

Move 1 *count 1*

■ *Boy LF back fallaway*

With your weight on the right foot, step backwards with your left foot, turning your body one-eighth to the left (the fallaway!). You'll notice your partner should be doing the opposite to you and you'll feel your left hand pull a little.

■ *Girl RF back fallaway*

With your weight on the left foot, step backwards with your right foot, turning your body more than the boy one-quarter to the right (the fallaway!). You'll notice your partner is doing the opposite and you should feel your right hand pull a little, remaining connected.

Move 2 *count 2*

■ *Boy weight forward to RF*

Transfer your weight forwards onto the right foot into PP and start to turn your partner to the left.

■ *Girl weight forward to LF*

Transfer your weight forwards onto the left foot into PP and think about being led to the left.

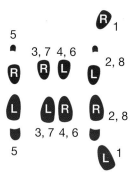

figure 20   fallaway rock

Moves 3–5 *counts 3 a 4*

■ *Boy LF side chassé LRL*

Step sideways with your left foot and chassé left, right, left, making an eighth of a turn to the right at the same time.

■ *Girl RF side chassé RLR*

Step sideways with your right foot and chassé right, left, right, making a quarter of a turn to the left at the same time in order to face your partner.

Moves 6–8 *counts 5 a 6*

■ *Boy RF side chassé RLR*

Step sideways with your right foot and chassé right, left, right, ending in a closed facing position.

■ *Girl LF side chassé LRL*

Step sideways with your left foot and chassé left, right, left, ending in a closed facing position.

Fallaway throwaway

The fallaway throwaway is basically the first five moves of the fallaway with a throwaway thrown in at the end. The throwaway is exactly what you would think it is – the boy throws the girl away from his body (not literally, but it feels like that).

This figure has eight steps and the rhythm goes like this: 1, 2, 3 a 4, 5 a 6.

Move 1 *count 1*

■ *Boy LF back fallaway*

With your weight on the right foot, step backwards with your left foot, turning your body one-eighth to the left (the fallaway!). You'll notice your partner should be doing the opposite to you and you'll feel your left hand pull a little.

■ *Girl RF back fallaway*

With your weight on the left foot, step backwards with your right foot, turning your body a quarter to the right (the fallaway!). You'll notice your partner is doing the opposite and you should feel your right hand pull a little, remaining connected.

Move 2 *count 2*

■ *Boy weight forward to RF*

Transfer your weight forwards onto the right foot into PP and start to turn your partner to the left.

■ *Girl weight forward to LF*

Transfer your weight forwards onto the left foot into PP and think about being led to the left.

Moves 3–5 *counts 3 a 4*

■ *Boy LF side chassé LRL*

Step sideways with the left foot and chassé left, right, left, making an eighth of a turn to the right at the same time.

> **Note:** On move 5, lower the hands and lean a little to the left.

■ *Girl RF side chassé RLR*

Step sideways with the right foot and chassé right, left, right, making a quarter of a turn to the left at the same time in order to face your partner.

> **Note:** On move 5, lower the hands and lean a little to the right.

Moves 6–8 *counts 5 a 6*

■ *Boy RF forward chassé RLR*

Step forwards with your right foot and chassé right, left, right, turning to the left, leading your partner to move away from you (this is the throwaway!). To do this, don't forget to release hold with your right hand.

■ *Girl LF back chassé LRL*

Step backwards with your left foot and chassé left, right, left, as you turn left (this is the throwaway!).

Link rock

The link rock has eight steps and the rhythm goes like this: 1, 2, 3 a 4, 5 a 6.

Move 1 *count 1*

■ *Boy LF back*

Start in the open facing position with your weight on the right foot, then step backwards with the left foot.

■ *Girl RF back*

Start in the open facing position with your weight on the left foot, then step backwards with the right foot.

Move 2 *count 2*

■ *Boy weight to RF*

Transfer your weight forwards onto the right foot.

■ *Girl weight to LF*

Transfer your weight forwards onto the left foot.

Moves 3–5 *counts 3 a 4*

■ *Boy LF forward chassé LRL*

Step forwards with the left foot and chassé left, right, left, as you lead your partner forwards, towards you.

■ *Girl RF forward chassé RLR*

Step forwards with the right foot and chassé right, left, right.

Moves 6–8 *counts 5 a 6*

■ *Boy RF side chassé RLR*

Step sideways with the right foot and chassé right, left, right, assuming the normal hold and ending in closed facing position.

■ *Girl LF side chassé LRL*

Step sideways with the left foot and chassé left, right, left, assuming the normal hold in a closed facing position.

Link and whip

This is the link and whip, and it links (fills in the missing two counts we spoke of earlier) and whips with a turn to the right, filling two complete bars of music.

There are ten steps in the link and whip for you to discover, and the rhythm of the full two bars of music is: 1 2 3 a 4, 1 2 3 a 4.

You can both start this in the open facing position.

Move 1 *count 1*

■ *Boy LF back*

With your weight on your right foot, step backwards with the left foot.

■ *Girl RF back*

With your weight on your left foot, step backwards with the right foot.

Move 2 *count 2*

■ *Boy weight forward to RF*

Transfer your weight forwards onto the right foot.

■ *Girl weight forward to LF*

Transfer your weight forwards onto the left foot.

Moves 3–5 *counts 3 a 4*

■ *Boy LF forward chassé LRL*

Step forwards with the left foot and chassé left, right, left, ending up with your left foot diagonally forward. You should have also just been leading your partner forwards and then assuming the normal hold.

■ *Girl RF forward chassé RLR*

Step forwards with the right foot and chassé right, left, right, ending up with your right foot forward between your partner's feet and assuming the normal hold.

Move 6 *count 1*

■ *Boy RF crosses behind LF*

Cross your right foot behind the left foot as you start to turn to the right.

■ *Girl LF forward*

Step forwards with the left foot towards your partner's right side as you also start to turn to the right.

Move 7 *count 2*

■ *Boy LF side*

Take a small step sideways with the left foot, enabling you to uncross your feet as you continue the turn to the right.

■ *Girl RF forward*

Take a small step forwards with the right foot, placing it between your partner's feet.

Moves 8–10 *counts 3 a 4*

■ *Boy RF side chassé RLR*

Take a really small step sideways with the right foot and chassé right, left, right, turning enough in order to end up in the fallaway position.

■ *Girl LF side chassé LRL*

Take a step sideways with the left foot and chassé left, right, left, turning to the right in order to end up in the fallaway position.

Change of place right to left

This figure has eight moves and the rhythm goes: 1, 2, 3 a 4, 5 a 6.

Move 1 *count 1*

■ *Boy LF back fallaway*

With your weight on the right foot, step backwards with the left foot, turning your body one-eighth to the left (the fallaway!). You'll notice your partner should be doing the opposite to you and you'll feel your left hand pull a little.

■ *Girl RF back fallaway*

With your weight on the left foot, step backwards with the right foot, turning your body a quarter to the right (the fallaway!). You'll notice your partner is doing the opposite and you should feel your right hand pull a little, remaining connected.

move 1

Move 2 *count 2*

■ *Boy weight forward to RF*

Transfer your weight forwards onto the right foot into PP and start to turn your partner to the left.

■ *Girl weight forward to LF*

Transfer your weight forwards onto the left foot into PP and think about being led to the left.

move 2

Moves 3–5 *counts 3 a 4*

■ *Boy LF side chassé LRL*

Step sideways with the left foot and chassé left, right, left, making an eighth of a turn to the right at the same time.

> **Note:** On count 5 raise your joined hands (your left hand) and start to turn your partner to her right.

■ *Girl RF side chassé RLR*

Step sideways with the right foot and chassé right, left, right, making a quarter of a turn to the left at the same time in order to face your partner.

> **Note:** On count 5 the boy is going to lift your joined hands (your right hand) and you will start to turn to the right.

move 3

move 5

move 4

Moves 6–8 *counts 5 a 6*

■ *Boy RF forward chassé RLR*
Please read carefully.

Step forwards with the right foot and chassé right, left, right. Here's the hard bit! During the chassé you are going to turn yourself to the left, at the same time you'll be leading your partner to finish her turn to the right under your raised left arm. As this happens, you release the hold you have with the right hand. You should now be in an open position ready to go into the following figure.

move 6

move 7

move 8

■ **Girl R turn chassé LRL**

Please read carefully, and don't move on until you've figured it out.

You should be continuing your turn to the right as you chassé left, right, left. During the chassés you will turn underneath the boy's left arm. He should release his right hand hold on you so you can turn freely to the right. When you've finished your turn, your left foot should be back, ready to go into the next figure.

Once you have tried and tested this and you feel supremely confident with it, as if you could do it in your sleep, you may move on to the change of place left to right. If you don't believe you have a handle on it just go back and work systematically through it again, you may have only missed one small point that's messing it up for you. Take a five-minute break and start again. I promise you it will be worth it in the long run. Don't get disheartened if something is going wrong. Downing tools is never the answer, learning is! Back on your feet, Latin lovers and ballroom babes!

Change of place left to right

This is simply the reverse of what you have just learnt, except you are going to begin with a link. The link is the back, replace, step that you did before, basically the first and second moves of the link rock or the link and whip.

Begin in the position you both ended up in after completing the change of places right to left, which is the figure just before this. You should both be in your open position. This figure has eight moves and the rhythm goes: 1, 2, 3 a 4, 5 a 6.

Move 1 *count 1*
■ *Boy LF back*
Start in the open facing position with your weight on the right foot, then step backwards with the left foot.

■ *Girl RF back*
Start in the open facing position with your weight on the left foot, then step backwards with the right foot.

Move 2 *count 2*
■ *Boy weight to RF*
Transfer your weight forwards onto the right foot.

■ *Girl weight to LF*
Transfer your weight forwards onto the left foot.

Moves 3–5 *counts 3 a 4*
■ *Boy LF to RF chassé LRL*
Don't close your feet together entirely but do close the left foot towards the right foot and chassé left, right, left. During the chassé you should be turning to the right and at the same time leading your partner to turn to the left underneath your raised left arm.

■ *Girl turn L chassé RLR*
Turn to the left underneath your partner's arm as you chassé right, left, right. At this point you should be in front of your partner with your back to him.

Moves 6–8 *counts 5 a 6*
■ *Boy RF forward chassé RLR*
Step forwards with the right foot and chassé right, left, right. Lead your partner into finishing her turn to the left, and lower the joined hands at the end of her turn.

■ *Girl LF back chassé LRL*
As you are continuing to turn to the left you step back with the left foot and chassé left, right, left. You'll be finishing off your turn to the left and ending with the joined hands lowered.

Note: You should both end up in an open facing position.

Change of hands behind back

This is one of the best moves in the jive – it looks amazing to novices and makes you feel like a true professional. Like all great things, this step may take a little study but once you've got it, you've got it for life!

This figure has eight moves and the rhythm goes like this: 1, 2, 3 a 4, 5 a 6.

You begin it in an open facing position and moves 1 and 2 are the same as moves 1 and 2 of the link.

move 1

move 2

Move 1 *count 1*

■ *Boy LF back*

Start in the open facing position with your weight on the right foot, then step backwards with the left foot.

■ *Girl RF back*

Start in the open facing position with your weight on the left foot, then step backwards with the right foot.

Move 2 *count 2*

■ *Boy weight to RF*

Transfer your weight forwards onto the right foot.

■ *Girl weight to LF*

Transfer your weight forwards onto the left foot.

Moves 3–5 *counts 3 a 4*

■ *Boy LF forward chassé LRL*

Step forwards with the left foot and chassé left, right, left. During this, place your right hand over your partner's right hand and at the same time release your hold with your left hand. You should be leading your partner forwards to your right side. This is the set up for the change of hands.

■ *Girl RF forward chassé RLR*

Step forwards with the right foot and chassé right, left, right. During this, you will move to your partner's right side and start your turn to the right.

move 3

move 5

Moves 6–8 *counts 5 a 6*

■ *Boy hand change chassé RLR*

Here's where the baton is passed, boys. Behind the back, change your partner's right hand into your left hand and at the same time you'll be turning your body to the left and dancing the chassés right, left, right. End with your right foot back.

■ *Girl turn R chassé LRL*

Chassé left, right, left, as you are turning to the right, behind your partner's back, ending up with your left foot back.

close-up of change of hands

move 6

Walks in promenade

The walks in promenade begin with the first and second moves of the fallaway rock so you should recognize them.

Here we have the normal eight steps and the rhythm goes like this: 1, 2, 3 a 4, 5 a 6.

Move 1 *count 1*

■ *Boy LF back fallaway*

With your weight on the right foot, step backwards with the left foot, turning one-eighth to the left (the fallaway!). You'll notice your partner should be doing the opposite to you and you'll feel your left hand pull a little.

- **Girl RF back fallaway**

With your weight on the left foot, step backwards with the right foot, turning a quarter of a turn to the right (the fallaway!). You'll notice your partner is doing the opposite and you should feel your right hand pull a little, remaining connected.

Move 2 *count 2*

- **Boy weight forward to RF**

Transfer your weight forwards onto the right foot into PP and start to turn your partner to the left.

- **Girl weight forward to LF**

Transfer your weight forwards onto the left foot into PP and think about being led to the left.

Moves 3–5 *counts 3 a 4*

- **Boy LF forward chassé LRL**

Step diagonally forwards with the left foot and chassé left, right, left, leading your partner to turn left.

- **Girl RF side chassé RLR**

Step sideways with the right foot and chassé right, left, right, making a quarter of a turn to the left.

Moves 6–8 *counts 5 a 6*

- **Boy RF forward chassé RLR**

This is slightly different so read carefully. Step forwards and across with the right foot to PP, then complete the chassé right, left, right, as you turn your partner to the right.

- **Girl LF forward chassé LRL**

Step forwards into PP with the left foot and chassé left, right, left, making a quarter of a turn to the right.

> **Note:** To end the figure, you can both chassé to the boy's left then back again to the boy's right.

> **Note:** There is an alternative to this step – after move 2 or move 8 you can substitute the chassé with single 'quick' steps and again these can be repeated. When dancing these single quick steps the girl needs to turn a quarter of a turn to the left then right and each turn is made towards the end of the previous beat of music, giving a twisting feel to it.

Kick ball change

The name of this step definitely goes with the moves you're actually doing as you kick your foot, land on the ball of the foot, and then change your weight. You can repeat it over and over, and it's also a great linking step to fill those two counts. You can use it instead of moves 1–2 of a link.

Only three more steps to learn and you're done – hoorah! If you haven't already, and you've been a gutless wonder, get on the telephone and find out about dance lessons at your local dance school. You've come this far and are now well equipped for the challenge so there's absolutely nothing to lose. Here's your final rhythm, enjoy it, it goes: 1 a 2!

Move 1 *count 1 = kick*

- **Boy flick LF forward**

Flick your left foot forwards.

- **Girl flick RF forward**

Flick your right foot forwards.

Move 2 *count a = ball*

- **Boy LF back**

Place your left foot just a little backwards, to be even with the heel of your right foot, staying on the ball of the foot.

- **Girl RF back**

Place your right foot just a little backwards, to be even with the heel of your left foot, staying on the ball of the foot.

Move 3 *count 2 = change*

- **Boy weight to RF**

Transfer your weight onto the right foot in place.

- **Girl weight to LF**

Transfer your weight onto the left foot in place.

Cool, you're done! Now go on and try these tasty and tempting combos.

amalgamations

Amalgamations for the jive

Routine one

Jive chassés to left and right

Fallaway rock

Fallaway throwaway

Link rock

Routine two

Change of places right to left

Change of places left to right

Link rock

Routine three

Link and whip

Walks in promenade

Kick ball change

Fallaway throwaway (moves 3–8)

> **Note:** Each routine can be repeated as many times as you desire.

Routine four

Jive chassés to left and right

Fallaway rock

Walks in PP

Kick ball change in PP × 2

Fallaway throwaway (moves 3–8)

Link rock

Make up your own!

to wrap up

You guys have done a great job getting through all these dances, and if you practise as much as you can, you will feel confident about going to a dance lesson. The dances in this book give you the basics and there are many more variations you can learn and look forward to dancing. I hope you've enjoyed the learning process and had some fun along the way. Why don't you practise the combos, get them polished, and go along to your local school and show off what you can do? It's time to put all that stuff into practice and never be frightened of social functions again. Thanks for taking the time to read the book and having the courage to put it into practice. Good luck, ballroom babes and Latin lovers, seize the day, dance and rule!

conclusion

I feel extremely fortunate to have had the opportunity to work on a show that has incited a world of people to be interested in dance. My time as a judge on the BBC's *Strictly Come Dancing* has been absolutely phenomenal. What I'm reminded of daily but have always known is that the human spirit has always, and forever will be lifted by music and dance, and that it really doesn't matter if you're not a great dancer or even a good dancer or, for that matter, if you're an absolutely terrible dancer, just to participate and enjoy the endorphin rush that dance can supply is all that counts. It's therefore my hope that since reading my book you will have mustered up enough courage to attend a dance lesson. There is so much to be gained, not only in the physical sense but also mentally and emotionally, from the experience of dance classes and one-on-one tuition. It is so very important that an experienced teacher guides and helps you to understand the true physical nature of the various dances through demonstration and correction, making that first brave step into the unknown easy and accessible.

Dance has been an enormous part of my life since I, too, plucked up enough courage to go and take my first class. I remember being so nervous and scared, not knowing what to expect and feeling so self-conscious with millions of questions going through my head – the entire 'what if?' range: What if I can't do it? What if everyone stares? What if I look a complete idiot? What if I fail? What if I just turn right around and go back home? Then it was too late, the door opened and my life changed from that moment on. It gave me strength and confidence and the will to be myself and to not worry about what anyone else thought. I'm very lucky to have dance in my life and to have worked with and choreographed the most incredible professional dancers worldwide, and I am so proud of the millions of people out there every day who have the guts to do and be what they want.

taking it further

If this book has inspired you to want to learn more about dance, there are many very informative magazines that supply loads of information about the various schools you can attend and organizations worldwide that support not only ballroom dance, but all forms of dance. One such magazine is the magazine of the Imperial Society of Teachers of Dancing (ISTD) dance examinations board, simply named *Dance*. It includes the latest news, reviews, examination information, faculties and a comprehensive course directory. Other magazines you may find interesting are *Dancesport* and *Dancing Times*. Here I have compiled a short list of schools, organizations and useful addresses that will help you on your journey into the wonderful world of dance.

Schools, organizations and useful addresses in the UK

Ann Lister School of Dance
70 Kenilworth Road, Scunthorpe,
North Lincolnshire DN16 1EY
Tel: 01724 338547

Anthony Clifford Studios Ltd.
66 Albert Road, Romford, Essex RM1 2PP
Tel: 01708 783576
Website: anthonycliffordstudios.co.uk

Ballroom Blitz (The Mitchell School of Dance)
10 Station Road, Kirton-in-Lindsey, Gainborough,
Lincolnshire DN21 4BB
Tel: 01652 649164

Betty Bouston Dance School
1 Bridge Court, Berkhamsted, Herts HP4 2JE
Tel: 01442 876780

British Association of Teachers of Dancing
23 Marywood Square, Glasgow, Scotland G41 2BP
Tel: 0141 423 4029
Website: **www.batd.co.uk**

British Competitors Dancesport Corporation
3 Dene Close, Poulner, Ringwood,
Hampshire BH24 1TB
Tel: 07798 728 955
Website: **www.britishcompetitors.com**

British Dance Council
Terpsichore House, 240 Merton Road,
South Wimbledon, London SW19 1EQ
Tel: 020 8545 0085
Website: **www.british-dance-council.org**

Diamond Dance Centre
Colin and Jacqui Donaldson's School
9 Queens Road, Farnborough, Hampshire GU14 6DJ
Tel: 01252 548748

Goodman Dance Centre
Len Goodman's School
3 Market Street, Dartford, Kent DA1 2DB
Tel: 01322 222508
Website: www.danceatgoodmans.com

Imperial Society of Teachers of Dancing
ISTD Dance Examinations Board
Imperial House, 22/26 Paul Street, London EC2A 4QE
Tel: 020 7377 1577
Website: www.istd.org

International Dance Shoes
Makers of fine quality, hand finished dance footwear.
11 Fingle Drive, I.O. Centre, Stonebridge,
Milton Keynes MK13 0AT
Tel: 01908 319937
Contact: Rashmi Patel
Email: sales@ids-danceshoes.co.uk
Website: www.ids-danceshoes.co.uk

International Dance Teachers' Association
International House, 76 Bennett Road,
Brighton, East Sussex BN2 5JL
Tel: 01273 685652
Website: www.idta.co.uk

Janet Clark Dance Studio
St. John Hall, 23 East Avenue, Walthamstow,
London E17 9NG
Tel: 0208 8013815

Lait Dance Club
Lodge Cottage, Bramford, Ipswich, Suffolk IP8 4AZ
Tel: 01473 743079

Margaret Preedy Dance Studios
33 Tonbridge Road, Maidstone, Kent ME16 8RX
Tel: 01622 688212

National Association of Teachers of Dancing
44–47 The Broadway, Thatcham, Berkshire RG19 3HP
Tel: 01635 868888
Website: www.natd.org.uk

Nigel Kirk 'Danceworks'
St. Pauls Parish Hall, St. Pauls Terrace, Low Moor,
Clitheroe, Lancashire BB7 2NU
Tel: 07930 432097
Tel: 01200 443791

Paradise Freeway Dance Education Centre
38 Cheddington Road, Muscliffe, Bournemouth,
Dorset BH9 3NB
Tel: 01202 516851

The Duesbury Aldred Dance Centre
Stapleford Community Centre, Cliff Hill Avenue,
Stapleford, Nottingham, NG9 7HD
Tel: 0115 9384688

The LP Dance Centre
Khyber Pass, Whitby, North Yorkshire YO21 3DQ
Tel: 01947 604516

The Professional Centre
1 Merringswell Road, Kentford, Newmarket,
Suffolk CB8 7QS
Tel: 01638 751175

The Windsor Ballroom School of Dance
5 Willow Street, Girlington, Bradford,
West Yorkshire BD8 9LT
Tel: 01274 488961

United Kingdom Alliance
Centenary House, 38/40 Station Road,
Blackpool FY4 1EU
Tel: 01253 408828
Website: www.ukadance.co.uk

International Organizations

American Ballroom Company
PO Box 453605, Miami, Fl. 33245/3605 USA
Tel: 1 305 442 1288

Australian Dancing Board
49 Links Road, Adross 6153, Western Australia
Tel: 9 364 3553

Canadian Dance Teacher's Association
94 Boulevard Lavesque, Pont Viau, Laval,
Quebec H7G ICI Canada
Tel: 514 669 6984

National Dance Council of America
24556 Mando Drive, Laguna Niguel, Ca 92677 USA
Tel: 1 714 643 9700

New Zealand Council of Ballroom Dancing
PO Box 37–342, Parnell, Auckland, New Zealand
Tel: 9 3034 650

South African National Council of Ballroom Dancing
7 Woodside, 8 Park Lane, Kloof,
Natal, South Africa 3610
Tel: 31 764 3732

what dance when?

Dance time warp

Prehistoric
Carol
Farandole
Fertility dances
Line dances
Medicine dances
Round dances

Classical antiquity
Bacchic dances/Dionysia
Hora
Kalamatianos
Morris dance
Sousta

Middle ages, twelfth to fourteenth centuries
Basse dance
Branle
Estampie
Danse macabre
European folk dances
Furlana
May dances
Saint Vitus's dance
Sword dances

Fifteenth century
Canaries
Hey
Hornpipe
Moresque
Sellenger's round

Sixteenth century
Allemande
Bergamasca
Bourree
Chaconne
Cinq pas
Country dance
Courante
Galliard
Measure
Pavane
Saraband
Sir Roger de Coverley
Trescone
La volta

Seventeenth century
Contredanse
Flamenco
Gavotte
Jig

Passacaglia
Rigaudon

Eighteenth century
Appalachian mountain dance
Contras (American country dance)
Carmagnole
Cotillion
Minuet
Passepied

1800–50
Bolero
Ecossaise
Galop
Lancers
Langaus
Mazurka
Polka
Polonaise
Quadrille
Schottische
Tsamikos
Waltz

1850–1900
Barn dance
Batuque

Cakewalk
Can can
Habañera
Milonga
Redowa
Round dances
Square dance
Two-step
Varsovienne

1900–10
Boston
Bunny hug
Buzzard lope
Camel walk
Crab
Eagle rock
Fanny bump
Fish tail
Funky butt
Grind
Grizzly bear
Horse trot
Itch
Kangaroo dip
Maxina
Maxcixe
Mooche
One-step
Slow drag
Squat
Tango
Turkey trot
Veleta

1910–20
Foxtrot

1920–30
Black bottom
Charleston
Lindy Hop
Quickstep
Rumba

Shimmy
Varisity drag

1930–40
Beguine
Big Apple
Boomps-a-daisy
Conga
Danzon
Guajira
Hokey-pokey
Jitterbug
Knees up
Lambeth walk
Palais glide
Paso doble
Samba

1940–50
Jitterbug
Jive

1950–60
Blue beat
Bop
Cha cha cha
Chicken
Clam
Fish
Fly
Madison
Mambo
Mashed potato
Merengue
Stroll
Twist

1960–70
Boogaloo
Bossa nova
Bug
Filly dog
Frug
Funky Broadway
Hitchhike

Hully-gully
Jerk
Monkey
Pachanga
Pony
Shake
Skate
Slop
Swim
Watusi

1970–80
Disco
Freestyling
Head banging
Jazz
Latin hustle
Ride-a-bike
Rope hustle
Slamming
Sling hustle
Street hustle
Tango hustle
The duke
The freak
The grapevine
The patty
West coast hustle

1980–90
Break dance
Bus stop
Line dancing
Moonwalk
Rodeo swing
Texas two-step

1990–present
B-styles
Capoeira
Electric boogie
Freestyle
Funk
Hip hop
Street

ballroom dance dictionary

Across the LOD Where a step is taken over or *across* the LOD.

Action The *type* of movement you use when you go into a step, for example, good and hot hip action. What you'll want is that hot hip action and for the beginner this can take a little time to master. Once you've got it however, there will be no stopping you! A good hip action is the result of good foot, ankle, knee and leg action, not the actual shaking or wiggling of the hips. The hips should simply occur naturally because of how your legs are moving.

Alemana turn This is a cool underarm turn in which the girl gets to be fierce and turns to the right under the right hand.

Alignment The direction that your body and feet are facing in relation to the room and the all-important LOD. It can also mean the direction of the movement. Your body should have 'proper alignment', basically lining up all your different body parts so they can move harmoniously together and make you look fabulous!

Amalgamation Just a fancy word for a dance routine or any combination of two or more steps or movements. I like calling them combos.

Amount of turn This just means how far your feet and body turn on a single step or between two consecutive steps. Normally turn is measured in fractions, for example, $\frac{1}{8}$, $\frac{1}{4}$ or $\frac{1}{2}$ of a full turn.

Apart Any dance position where the boy and girl are not in a hold together or are dancing without touching one another.

Appel An accented movement in place, where the body weight is placed dramatically and boldly onto a flat foot and to give you more of an idea – it's like what kids do when they want something they are not allowed to have and stamp their feet! The paso doble is full of them – just think Spanish. An Appel would normally indicate the start of a strong directional movement.

Arabesque This is a cool position that takes lots of training and is used a lot in classical dance. It's a position of the body where your free leg is extended straight behind the body and lifted off the floor.

Arch The nicest part of the foot, between the ball and the heel, which when the foot is pointed, makes an *arched* shape.

Argentine tango It's not covered in this book but is a style of tango that most people will recognize as it's full of passion and lots of weaving and flicking leg movements. It originated in Buenos Aires.

Attitude A body position where the free leg is raised with the knee bent and has nothing to do with whether you have a good or bad one!

Axis Dancers use this so that they don't fall over during a turn. You have to imagine a vertical line that runs either through the centre of the body, through one of its sides, or outside of the body altogether, around which the body turns.

Backing How the alignments are described to specify movement that is backward. For example: *Backing LOD* or *Backing DC*.

Back-to-back position Just as it suggests, a dance position where the boy and girl face away from each other.

Balance If you've been on the merry-go-round for too long you won't have any of this. Technically it's the correct distribution of body weight between the feet or over the standing foot.

Ball Not a round object used in games or a formal social function, but a dance term used to describe the landing of body weight onto the ball of the foot, the padded area between the arch of the foot and the toes. You'll see it mentioned a lot in the quickstep section. A 'ball' step is taken without the heel in contact with the floor.

Ball change A series of two consecutive steps, the first step being taken with the ball of the foot only and the change part is when you transfer or change your weight. The rhythm is usually syncopated.

Ball-flat A ball-flat step is taken first with the ball of the foot in contact with the floor, and then with the whole foot flat on the floor.

Ball-heel A ball-heel step is taken first with the ball of the foot in contact with the floor, and then with the whole foot flat. When the weight is released from a ball-heel step, the toe will release from the floor while the heel maintains contact.

Bar Music is measured in units that represent a group of consecutive beats. The number of beats in a bar is measured by the time signature. For instance in the waltz there are three beats to each bar of music and in the rumba there are four beats to each bar of music.

Basic figure A series of steps that make up the basis of a standardized dance – not whether you have a 25 inch waist!

Beat Like a heartbeat that doesn't stop, a beat is a pulse in the music that is not dissimilar to the *Titanic* theme song, *My Heart Will Go On* and on and on and so on! You see, it's a continuous pulse within which the rhythms are formed. It can also be an isolated, single pulse in the music.

Beat value This is how long the beat lasts for. For example: the beat value of a 'slow' count is two beats and a 'quick' count would be one beat.

Body contact Just as the term suggests, it's the point of physical contact between a boy and girl's body or for that matter a boy and boy's or girl and girl's body when in closed, promenade, or outside partner position.

Body rise The body rise is the result of the bracing of the muscles of the legs creating elevation of the body. In layman's terms, when you straighten your knees your body rises up – creating body rise.

Body turn The body can turn even if the feet are going in a different direction and it's generally the amount of turn of the body we talk about if different from the feet.

Body weight Not the percentage of fat you have compared to lean muscle tissue, but a term we use to suggest that one's weight can travel from one leg to the other by shifting your body weight through your centre.

Brush The action of closing the moving foot to the standing foot, without changing weight, between steps and certainly not the one you use for cleaning the toilet or grooming your hair.

Carriage Your carriage does await but won't turn into a pumpkin at midnight thankfully as this term relates to the position of the upper body while in dance position.

Centre The invisible line that runs through the body which gives you your centre of balance, also refers to the centre of the room or dance floor. In the alignments, the centre is determined to be the direction exactly opposite the wall.

Cha Cha Cha The cha cha cha is a cool Latin dance from Cuba. It's based on the rhythm of the triple mambo consisting of two slow steps and three quick steps hence the rhythm 'slow slow cha cha cha' or 'cha cha cha slow slow'. Just the very words have a suggestion of bongo beats going mad, tantalizing timbales with mental maracas shaking the house down. The time signature for the cha cha cha is 4/4. That means four beats to every bar of music.

Change of weight Mine changes daily but in the dance world it means the full transfer of body weight from one foot to the other.

Chassé It's French and pronounced *shas-say*. A chassé is a series of two or three consecutive lateral steps, where the feet are closed on the second step. A sliding step in which one foot *chassés* and displaces the other.

Choreography A creation or composition of steps or movements, which make up a dance or dance routine that is set to music.

Closed facing position A dance position in the normal hold, where the partners face each other.

Closed finish The last part of a figure that ends with feet together.

Combination This is another name for amalgamation and the full version of the slang word combo. It's a mixture of different patterns or choreography, or the act of mixing them.

Connection Can be a physical point of contact or a way of communicating with your partner.

Contra body movement (CBM) It's what your body does in relation to your feet and is used to start turns. It's basically your body turning the opposite hip and shoulder towards the direction of the moving leg. Also known as contrary body movement position (CBMP).

Contra position This is the dance position where the boy and girl are both moving towards each other's left or right side, both using the same foot.

Control Without balance and stability throughout the body while you are dancing, your life in dance would be limited. You need great control over your body when you dance.

Corté This is a Spanish word meaning 'cut' and the name given to several steps in ballroom dancing. You will have learnt it in the tango but here it is known as a back corté .The back corté is a figure used if the guy is travelling backwards to the LOD and wants to go in a forward direction. It consists of four moves and the rhythm used is SQQS.

Counterpart The corresponding part to a figure danced by the partner.

Counter promenade position A V-shaped dance position with the girl on the boy's left side.

Counter weight Tension applied to a connection through the opposition of the partners' body weight.

Cucarachas A basic international figure consisting of side steps to the left and right. This move is deliciously simple and named after one of my most favourite insects, the cockroach! It's a useful 'holding pattern' dance until you decide what step may follow. It gets its name from the Spanish word, 'cucaracha' which means cockroach.

Cut time A term for the time signature of 2/4, representing two beats to every bar of music. The samba and tango are examples of music written in cut time, and it's notated in the time signature by a 'C' with a slash through it. Also called *alla breve*.

Dance position The position of the dancers in relationship to each other when dancing.

Dancesport The official name given to the sport of competitive ballroom dancing.

Développé (Dev-lo-pay) An 'unfolding' of the leg, mainly used in ballet, where the free foot is drawn up to the knee of the supporting leg, and then extended (or developed, unfolded) until the leg is completely straight. It's really difficult, as you need very strong and supple muscles.

Diagonal movement A movement that travels sideways and forward or back at the same time.

Directional movement This is the direction that you are going to be dancing in, a movement facing or backing a specific direction. There are three different directional movements, lateral (sideways), progressive (forwards or backwards) and diagonal (a combination of both).

Downbeat This isn't a mood swing or your partner showing or expressing pessimism and hopelessness, but simply refers to the very first beat in a bar of music. It is also the downward movement made by a conductor to indicate the downbeat of a bar of music.

Drop A fabulous dance move when the girl's body weight becomes supported by the boy, while at least one part of her body remains in contact with the floor, normally the foot. Girl's, you really have to trust your partner for this one!

Dynamics The different levels in the qualities of dancing, such as speed, mood and intensity. It can also mean the different levels of loudness and softness in a piece of music, and the way in which a performer reproduces them in performance. It's the dynamics in the dancers' performance that gives them the edge.

English style An internationally recognized style of ballroom dancing.

Expression The communication of character and emotion displayed by the dancer. Also, the face you might pull in order to put passion in your tango!

Facing ... How the alignments are described to specify the alignment of the body, for example *Facing LOD* (Line of Dance), *Facing DC* (Diagonally Centre), *FW* (Facing Wall), *FC* (Facing Centre).

Fallaway position A V-shaped dance position similar to promenade position (PP), but with the boy and girl stepping backwards.

Fan An enthusiastic admirer of a celebrity or public performer but also a basic figure used in the rumba and cha cha cha.

Fan position An opened out dance position where the boy and girl stand at right angles, girl on the boy's left side. The boy holds the girl's right hand in his left hand.

Figure This is the name given to a standardized step pattern, which, together with other patterns, makes up the basis of a dance and so, nothing to do with how slim you are!

Flat The foot is flat to the floor, not an apartment in Catford.

Flex When I talk about a flexed knee that just means to bend your knee with your weight on it like in the tango. It can also mean an inclined position of the foot that is achieved when the heel is still in contact with the floor, but the ball is not.

Flick A staccato or sharp extension of the lower leg. You normally call a flick, a kick.

Floor craft Well, it's not dissimilar to witchcraft, as you need to develop a 'sixth sense' if you want to stay out of hospital. You must have your wits about you if there are more people on the dance floor other than you and your partner, and even if you're the only couple dancing, it can be dangerous as there are walls, tables, chairs, wine and beer bottles at weddings and all sorts of other unexpected obstacles you both may crash into or slip on. This is why you need good floorcraft, in order to dodge other couples and surprise obstacles while remaining in control and looking graceful. You also need to be able to anticipate the direction other couples may take and have a 'sixth sense' about which route they may take. Basically you must follow certain rules and go with the traffic flow. We all know what could happen if you drove your car up the wrong side of the road, don't we?

Following This is the worst bit for the girls. The girl has to react to the movements and signals given by the boy, through either physical or visual communication. Whatever mess the boy makes of the dance, it's the girl's responsibility to follow him, right or wrong! It's sort of like marriage – sickness and in health, richer, poorer, better, worse, and it shouldn't end in divorce if you are both aware of one another and take equal responsibility for your weight and balance. The girl must carry herself and her weight in such a way that doesn't make her partner feel as if he is dragging her around the dance floor.

Foot positions The placement of the feet relative to each other for example: *LF Forward*, *RF Side* and so on.

Foot pressure The application of pressure to the floor through the free foot placing partial body weight on it.

Foot rise The ups and downs of the body are created through the use of the ankles and by lifting or rising up onto the balls of the feet.

Footwork The part of the foot in contact with the floor on each step.

Foxtrot A smooth dance named after a music hall performer who went by the name of Harry Fox, who performed a trotting dance to ragtime at the Ziegfeld Follies way back in 1914, characterized by smooth, walking style movements and the combination of Quick's and Slows.

Frame The position of the arms and body in dance position. For example: in the normal hold, the boy creates a frame that the girl moves into.

Free foot, leg or hand The foot or leg that doesn't hold all the body weight. It's the foot that's available to step onto or the hand that is not holding the partner.

Heel The part of the foot directly below the ankle and behind the arch. You will see this term a lot in the quickstep chapter, where I have mentioned the footwork.

Heel lead The heel is first placed down in contact with the floor and then with the whole foot flat to the floor. You lead with the heel.

Heel turn Here you do a turn on the heel of the foot. It's used in the zig zag step in the quickstep. The movement starts with a backwards step (ball-heel). The turn begins when the free foot closes to the foot with weight on it and held parallel throughout the turn. The weight then transfers to the closing foot at the end of the turn.

Hesitation A moment in which progression or travel around the room is held up for a bit and technically known as 'checked'. The weight is held on the foot that has the weight on it for one or more beats.

Hip action A good hip action is the result of good foot, ankle, knee and leg action, not the actual shaking or wiggling of the hips. The hips should simply occur naturally because of how your legs are moving.

Hockey stick A basic figure used in international rumba and cha cha cha. It's in the rumba and it's move 4 count 2. The boy takes a small step back onto the right foot and turns a bit to the right leading his girl past him, raising his hand above her head as she does so. The girl walks forwards onto the left foot and starts to turn to the left in front of the boy. This forward step for the girl is the part of the hockey stick shape that curves at the end of the stick. Hence the name!

Inside foot Your inside foot is the foot that's closest to your partner when you are in promenade, outside partner, or side-by-side position.

Instep This isn't an 'in' or 'fashionable' step, but is the part of the foot which is on the inside edge, between the ball and the heel.

Jive Originally brought to the sunny shores of the UK by those wild and crazy American GI's during the Second World War. Even with its fast tempo, the Jive is still danced in triple-rhythm. The jive is a non-progressive dance, which means that it doesn't move around the dance floor but instead stays pretty much in place.

Jitterbug An older style of swing danced in single-rhythm, to very fast big band jazz music of the thirties and forties.

Kick ball change This name definitely goes with the moves you're actually doing as you *kick* your foot, land on the *ball* of the foot and then *change* your weight, normally taken in a syncopated rhythm, such as 1 and 2.

Lateral movement Simply a sideways movement.

Latin hip action The characteristic movement of the hips found in the Latin dances.

Latin walks Forward or backward walks with hot Latin hip action.

Leading and following The boy is responsible for leading from one figure to another and it's the girl's job to follow.

Lindy Hop A form of swing that was named after Charles Lindberg.

Line A line that can be imaginary, like the LOD or the line created by the positioning of the body.

Line of Dance Abbreviated (LOD). An imaginary line that is drawn anticlockwise around the dance floor or room in which you are intending to dance. It's the motorway you'll be dancing down and loads of imaginary roads run off it. On your left is the **centre** of the room, normally where the chandelier is fixed. When you have discovered the **centre** of the room, look to your right and you should see a wall of some description. This is the **wall**. Your motorway is the area between the **centre** and the **wall**. It is within this area that you dance in an anticlockwise direction around the dance floor.

Lowering The lowering of the body to the heel and whole foot after being up on your toes or the balls of your feet, achieved through the use of your ankles and feet.

Measure As opposed to the measures in cooking or units of alcohol this measure is a unit of music that represents a group of consecutive beats. The time signature tells you the amount of beats in a bar or measure. It can also represent a whole phrase of a dance, not dissimilar to the rhythm or meter of a piece of poetry.

Modern style ballroom The old term for what's known now as the international standard style of ballroom dancing.

Moving Not house or anything to do with whether you've been moved by something visual, but moving in the direction toward which the body is travelling.

Moving foot or leg The foot or leg that is active and doesn't carry the body weight.

Musicality Having good musicality in dance is essential as it's the ability to understand and interpret music in a way that is artistically expressive and technically correct – being able to hear and have a good sense of the rhythms and beats in the music.

Natural opposite Just another name for when you and your partner mirror one another with the steps.

Natural turn A turn to the right.

Open figure Any figure without a closing or chassé action, which involves the continuous passing of the feet.

Open finish The final step of a figure that ends with the feet passing.

Open position Any dance position where the boy and girl stand apart, without taking a closed position dance hold.

Open facing position

Left hand to right hand hold

In this hold, you will be in an open position, a little apart from your partner. The boy takes the girls right hand in his left hand and the free arm is normally extended to the side at waist height

Right hand to left hand hold
This is the same as the hold above, but the girl's left hand is held in the boy's right hand.

Opposition When you and your partner dance in opposition, you move in the opposite direction of each other.

Outside foot The foot that is the furthest away from your partner when in the promenade, outside partner, or side-by-side positions.

Outside partner position (OPP) You can see a close-up photo of this position on p.15. It's a step that is taken forward by the boy or girl that doesn't follow the partner's opposite foot but is taken to the right or left, outside the partner.

Paso Doble A very dramatic Spanish style dance, with a 2/4 time signature, with the boy portraying the matador in a bullfight and the girl as the cape. It's what the characters Fran and Scott danced for the finale in Baz Lurmann's movie *Strictly Ballroom*.

Pattern A small group of individual steps or movements.

Pencil turn I did loads of these in *West Side Story*! It's a turn on one foot, with the free foot held next to the standing foot in a parallel first position. Not particularly easy!

Phrase A musical phrase is a sequence of notes that form a unit of melody within a piece of music. In dance, a phrase is a short sequence of dance steps or movements.

Pivot A turn on the ball of one foot with the other foot being kept in front or behind in CBMP.

Point An extended position of the foot where the toe or ball is still in contact with the floor and the heel is lifted. Can also be directional: an instruction referring to the alignment of the feet, for example: pointing your foot along the LOD.

Poise The position of the body in relation to the feet.

Posture The way you hold your body and carry yourself. Good posture is achieved by vertically aligning the head, shoulders, abdomen, and hips.

Progressive movement Movement that travels forward or backward.

Promenade position (PP) You both have to create a V-shape with your torsos. The boy is facing the front and the girl turns her body to the right. Don't exaggerate this position and make sure your bodies remain in contact with each other on the boy's right side and the girl's left side. See the photo on p.14.

Quick A count which is equal to one beat of music, exactly 1/2 the time of a 'Slow'.

Quickstep An English style ballroom dance that is full of body swing movements and syncopated hops, kicks, skips, lock steps and chassés all at major speeds.

Reverse turn A turn to the left.

Rhythm This is the regular pattern of beats and emphasis in a piece of music – the pulse or beat created by the various musical and percussive instruments playing a piece of music. If you ain't got it, get it quick!

Rise and fall The up and down feeling of the movement as you move through the steps. Rise and fall is like life, it's full of ups and downs, but unlike life, you can control when your up and when your down. For example in the waltz you step forward on the heel then rise to the toe; start to rise up at the end of step one then continue to rise on steps two and three, then at the end of step three, you simply lower or fall.

Rock Step A transfer or replacement of weight back and forth from one foot to the other, in place.

Rumba Known as the dance of love, this horny Latin American dance has a time signature of 4/4, and is characterized by it's sensual, provocative movements, it's hot'n'horny hip action, flirtatious and teasing role play between the boy and girl.

Samba An extremely rhythmical Brazilian party dance with a 2/4 time signature. The samba is noted for it's distinct style of movement, which has loads of hot hip action and that incredible samba bounce.

Samba bounce Samba bounce is rhythmical and achieved by the continuous flexing and straightening of the knees. There are two types of bounce, basic and alternative.

1. **Basic bounce (BB)** On the step: the knees are flexed; between the step: the knees are straightened.

2. **Alternative basic bounce (ABB)** Count one; on the first step: the knees are flexed. Count a; on the second step: the knees are straightened. Count two; on the third step: the knees are flexed.

Shadow position A dance position where the boy and girl are facing the same direction. One partner would either be directly in front of the other, or offset slightly to the left or right.

Side-by-side position

Left Side-by-Side (LS×S)
This is used loads in the rumba and cha cha cha. It's also used in the jive! It where the girl is on the guy's left side with you both facing the same way.

Right Side-by-Side (RS×S)
This is the same but reversed, where the girl is on the guy's right side facing the same way!

Slow A count equal to two beats of music, exactly twice the time of a 'Quick'.

Slow waltz A dance with a 3/4 time signature that developed from the much faster Viennese waltz. Rise and fall and circular movement characterize the slow waltz.

Social foxtrot Named after a music hall performer who went by the name of Harry Fox, who performed a trotting dance to ragtime at the Ziegfeld Follies way back in 1914, Mr Fox's trot caught on. It was brought from America to the UK in 1915 and originally was quite a wild dance with loads of hops and kicks until the Brits got their hands on it, calming it right down and making it smoother. The beauty and versatility of the foxtrot is you can dance to loads of different music, anything with a 2/4 or 4/4 time signature.

Spin A very fast turn.

Spotting Spotting stops you getting dizzy when you have a load of turns to do. What happens is this; during the turn you focus on a fixed point turning the head at a faster speed than the body.

Step The foot is picked up off the floor and placed forward, back or side onto the floor changing the weight from one foot to the other. Also a term for a group of steps like the hockeystick in the rumba.

Stretch To extend a limb or muscle to full length.

Supporting leg or foot The leg or foot that takes all or some of the body weight.

Stride The length of a step.

Sway Sway is simply the tilting of the body. What you do is sway away from the reaching foot and sway toward the closing foot. Sway can be used on all turns except spins because they're just too fast to sway safely. The main thing about sway is to incline the body towards the centre of the turn.

Swinging action The action of the body weight swinging from foot to foot.

Swivel A turn on the ball of one foot.

Syncopate The modification of a musical rhythm by shifting the accent to a weaker beat of the bar. Check out the Syncopated New York on p.161!

Tango In the international ballroom styles the tango is danced to a 2/4 time signature. Argentina cracked it first and you'll recognize it by its dramatic and staccato head movements.

Tempo The speed of a piece of music or a dance, measured in beats per minute. Its really important that the speed or tempo is right for the specific dance you want to do you certainly don't want to be doing a slow foxtrot at 50 bars a minute as it will resemble a quickstep! The foxtrot should be set at 30 bars a minute.

Time signature A sign used in music to show meter, represented by a fraction in which the upper figure shows beats per measure and the lower figure shows each beat's time value.

Toe One of five wiggly things that hang off the end of your feet, term used to express what part of the foot is used at any one particular time like 'lead with the heel, not with the toe!' In footwork descriptions toe can also mean stepping onto the ball of the foot with the heel off the floor. For example: rise up on your toes or LF toe would simply mean step onto the ball of your left foot with your heel up off the floor.

Toe heel The footwork used on a lowering action or backwards step.

Toe release Releasing the toe (ball of foot) from the floor while stepping onto the heel on a backwards walk.

Top line The line created by the upper part of the body.

Turn A rotational type movement left or right.

Turned out A foot position, where the toes point outwards, away from each other.

Underarm turn A turn that occurs under joined hands above the head.

Variation Variations are step patterns that have been modified and are either non-standard or non-syllabus and can be individual to each couple.

Waltz A ballroom style dance that first developed in Vienna as a fast paced dance to the Strauss music of the time, now called the Viennese waltz and later developed into the slow or social waltz. The time signature for the waltz is 3/4, which simply means, it has three beats to every bar. That means you only count up to 3, instead of 4 as in all the other dances. The down beat or first beat of the bar is pronounced 1 2 3, 1 2 3 etc...

West Coast Swing A swing dance characterized by its smooth and linear style that has a time signature of 4/4, that's four beats to the bar.

Whip Yes, horses and bulls have been on the receiving end of it but in dance terms it's a figure that whips the girl from one side of the boy to the other, and back again.

bibliography

Ballroom Dancing, Alex Moore, seventh edition, 1963, London, Sir Isaac Pitman & Sons Ltd.

Ballroom Dancing, The Imperial Society of Teachers of Dancing, Hodder & Stoughton, 1983.

The Ballroom Dancing Annual 1950, A. H. Franks, John Dillworth Ltd, London, 1950.

A Concise History of Latin American Dancing in the United Kingdom, Irene Evans, 1992.

Let's Dance, Paul Bottomer, Lorenze Books 1998, Anness Publishing Limited, 2000, London.

Let's Dance, Peter Buckman, Paddington Press 1978, London.

index

abbreviations 5
Alemana turn
    cha cha cha 167–8, 171
    rumba 112–15, 118
amalgamations
    cha cha cha 171
    jive 192
    quickstep 74
    samba 146
    social foxtrot 53
    waltz 38
ankle rolls 10
Argentina, and the tango 78
Astaire, Fred 122

back basic
    cha cha cha 157–8, 171
    rumba 102–3, 118
back corté
    foxtrot 49
    tango 87–9
backward walk
    rumba 99
    tango 80
ball 3
ballroom dances 21–93
    holds 12–14
    shoes 8
    see also quickstep; social foxtrot; tango;
        waltz
Ballroom Dancing Annual 1
body weight 3
Bota fogos steps (samba) 138–43

to promenade/counter promenade
        position 138–41, 146
    travelling 142–3
bounce action (samba) 124
Brazil, and the samba 122
brush 3
Buenos Aires, and the tango 78

Calloway, Cab 176
centre 3
    of the room 6
cha cha cha 148–73
    Alemana turn 167–8, 171
    amalgamations 171
    basic movement
        back 157–8, 171
        forward 154–6, 171
        in place 152–3
        turning left 159
    the fan 165–6, 171
    hand to hand 163–4
    history 150
    the hockey stick 166–7, 171
    hold 18, 151
    music 150
    New York 160–2, 171
    right foot and left foot chassé 152
    shoulder to shoulder 168–9, 171
    spot turns 162–3, 171
    there and back step 169–70
    time steps 164–5, 171
    see also chassés
change of place right to left (jive) 182–6

the Charleston 58
chassés
    cha cha cha
        Alemana turn 167–8
        basic movement turning left 159
        left foot 152
        New York 160–1
        right foot 151–2
        shoulder to shoulder 168–9
    jive 177, 179, 192
        change of place left to right 187
        change of place right to left 184–6
        hand change behind back 189–90
        left and right 179
        link and whip 182, 183
        right 179
    quickstep
        progressive chassé 60–4
        reverse turn with a chassé ending 69, 74
    social foxtrot 50, 51–2
close contact hold (rumba) 99
closed promenade (tango) 89–90
clothing 8
corta jaca 123, 143–4, 146
Cuban folk dance, and the rumba 98
cucaracha (rumba) 104–5
    side cucaracha to the left 104, 118
    side cucaracha to the right 105, 118

DC (Diagonally Centre) 7
Dirty Dancing 24
downbeat 3
DW (Diagonally to the Wall) 7

elbow circles 9
Ellington, Duke 176
Evita 79

fallaway position 17
fallaway rock (jive) 180, 192
fallaway throwaway (jive) 181, 192
the fan
   cha cha cha 165–6, 171
   rumba 109–10, 118
films 1
   Flying Down to Rio 122
   and the tango 78–9
   West Side Story 105
floorcraft (waltz) 25
flow, and the waltz 25
Flying Down to Rio 122
follow through 3
foot positions 7
footwork 3
forward basic
   cha cha cha 154–6, 171
   rumba 100–1, 118
forward lock step (quickstep) 65–7
forward walk
   rumba 99
   tango 80
The Four Horsemen of the Apocalypse
   78–9
Fox, Harry 42
foxtrot *see* social foxtrot
Franks, A.H. 1, 203–5
FW (Facing Wall) 7

Gauchos, and the tango 78
Goodman, Benny 176

hamstring stretches 10
hand change behind back (jive) 188–90
hand to hand
   cha cha cha 163–4
   rumba 117, 118
hesitation change (waltz) 33–4, 38
hip exercises 10
history of dances 198–9
   cha cha cha 150
   jive 176
   quickstep 58
   rumba 98
   samba 122
   social foxtrot 42
   tango 78–9
   waltz 24–5
the hockey stick
   cha cha cha 166–7, 171
   rumba 111–12, 118

holds 12–19
   ballroom 12–14
      quickstep 59
      social foxtrot 43
      tango 79
      waltz 26
   Latin American 15–19
      cha cha cha 151
      jive 177
      rumba 18, 19, 99
      samba 124

Imperial Society of Teachers of Dancing
   25, 42, 79
instep 3

jazz age 58
jitterbug 176
jive 176–93
   amalgamations 192
   change of hands behind back 188–90
   change of place
      left to right 187, 192
      right to left 182–6, 192
   fallaway rock 180, 192
   fallaway throwaway 181, 192
   getting rhythm in body and hands 177–8
   history 176
   hold 177
   kick ball change 191, 192
   link rock 181–2, 192
   link and whip 182–3, 192
   music 177
   walks in promenade 190–1, 192
   see also chassés
Johnson, Ken 'snakehips' 202
Jorrin, Enrique 150

kick ball change (jive) 191, 192
Kilpatrick, Pat 204
knee bends 10

Laban, Rudolf 202
Latin American dances 95–193
   cha cha cha 148–73
   holds 15–19
   rumba 97–119
   samba 120–47
   shoes for 8
Lindberg, Charles 176
lindy hop 176
link into closed promenade (tango) 89–90,
   91
link rock (jive) 181–2, 192
link and whip (jive) 182–3, 192
lock step (quickstep) 65–7, 74
LOD (Line of Dance) 6–7

Louis XIII, King of France 134
Luhrmann, Baz 79

Madonna 79
Maxixe dance 122
measure 3
Minneli, Liza 105
Miranda, Carmen 122, 138
Moore, Alex 204
Moulin Rouge 1, 79
music
   cha cha cha 150
   jive 177
   quickstep 59
   rumba 98
   social foxtrot 42–3
   tango 79
   waltz 25
musicals 1
My One and Only 176

natural basic (samba) 125, 146
natural pivot turn with corner (quickstep)
   70–1
natural turn with hesitation (quickstep) 68,
   74
natural turn (waltz) 28–31, 38
neck stretches 9
the New York
   cha cha cha 160–2, 171
      syncopating 161–2
   rumba 105–8, 118
New York World Fair (1939) 122

O'Connor, Caroline 1, 79
open reverse turn closed finish (tango)
   86–7
opening out right and left (rumba) 116,
   118
operas 1
organizations worldwide 198–9

Pacino, Al 79
physical condition 2
pivot step (quickstep) 70–1, 74
progressive basic (samba) 130
progressive chassé (quickstep) 60–4
promenade position
   ballroom dances 14
      social foxtrot 50, 51–2, 53
      waltz 36
   Latin dances 16
      jive 190–1
      samba 133, 138–41, 146
      tango 89–90
   see also walks in promenade
prostitutes, and the tango 78

quickstep 56–75
  amalgamations 74
  heel leads 59
  history 58
  hold 59
  lock step 65–7, 74
  music 59
  natural pivot turn with corner 70–1, 74
  natural turn with hesitation 68, 74
  zig zag 71–3, 74
  see also chassés

reaches 9
reverse basic (samba) 127
reverse turn
  samba 144–5, 146
  waltz 32–3, 38
Rio de Janeiro carnival 122
rock turn (tango) 80–4, 91
rock'n'roll 176
Rogers, Ginger 122
rumba 97–119
  Alemana turn 112–15, 118
  amalgamations 118
  back basic 102–3, 118
  backward walk 99
  basic 99
  cucaracha 104–5, 118
  the fan 109–10, 118
  forward basic 100–1, 118
  forward walk 99
  hand to hand 117
  history 98
  the hockey stick 111–12, 118
  hold 18, 19, 99
  hot action 98–9
  music 98
  the New York 105–8, 118
  opening out right and left 116, 118
  shoes 99
  side step 104
samba 120–47
  alternative basic
    natural 126
    reverse 127–8
  amalgamations 146
  Bota fogos 138–43, 146
  bounce action 124
    alternative basic bounce 124, 134
  corta jaca 123, 143–4, 146
  history 122
  hold 124
  music 122–3
  natural basic 125, 146

progressive basic 130
reverse basic 127
reverse turn 144–5, 146
side basic
  with alternative basic bounce 129–30
  with basic bounce 128
voltas 134–7
  travelling left 134–6, 146
  travelling right 137, 146
walks in promenade 133, 146
whisk
  to left 132, 146
  to right 131–2, 146
Saturday Night Fever 24
Scent of a Woman 79
schools 196–7
Second World War 202
shake out 10
shoes 8, 99
shoulder rolls 9
shoulder to shoulder (cha cha cha) 168–9, 171
show tango 79
side basic (samba)
  with alternative basic bounce 129–30
  with basic bounce 128
side step (rumba) 104
Silvester, Victor 203, 204
Sinatra, Frank 105
social foxtrot 40–55
  amalgamations 53
  back corté 49, 53
  basic quarter turns 43–4, 53
  entry step 50, 53
  history 42
  hold 43
  music 42–3
  natural pivotal turn 44–6, 53
  promenade walk and chassé 50, 51–2, 53
  reverse pivot turn 47
  side step 48, 53
spot turns (cha cha cha) 162–3, 171
Strictly Come Dancing 195
Swayzee, Patrick 24

tango 76–93, 80–90
  amalgamations 91
  back corté 87–9
  basic reverse turn 85, 91
  de salon 79
  front view hold 14
  history 78–9
  hold 79
  link into closed promenade 89–90, 91

music 79
open reverse turn closed finish 86–7
orillero 79
rock turn 80–4, 91
shoes 8
styles of 79
walk 79–80
Tango Argentina 79
tendon stretches 10
there and back step (cha cha cha) 169–70
time steps (cha cha cha) 164–5, 171
toe 4
toe raises 10
travelling Bota fogos (samba) 142–3
travelling voltas (samba)
  left 134–6, 146
  right 137, 146
Travolta, John 24

Valentino, Rudolf 78–9
Viennese waltzes 24–5
voltas (samba) 134–7, 146

walks in promenade
  jive 190–1, 192
  samba 133, 146
  social foxtrot 50, 51–2
wall of the room 6
waltz 23–39
  amalgamations 38
  floorcraft 25
  hesitation change 33–4, 38
  history 24–5
  hold 26
  left foot closed change 28, 38
  modern (diagonal) 25
  music 25
  natural turn 28–31, 38
  outside change 34
  reverse turn 32–3, 38
  right foot closed change 27, 38
  rise and fall 26
  sway 26
  Viennese (quick) 25
  the whisk 35–7, 38
warm-up techniques 2, 9–10
West End London shows 1, 176
West Side Story 105
whisk
  samba 131–2, 146
  waltz 35–7, 38

Ziegfeld Follies 42, 58
zig zag (quickstep) 71–3, 74